C0 BPU 991

THE HISTORY OF ADVERTISING

40 MAJOR BOOKS IN FACSIMILE

Edited by

HENRY ASSAEL
C. SAMUEL CRAIG
New York University

A
GARLAND
SERIES

ADVERTISING
AND SELLING
ABROAD

F. L. ELDRIDGE

GARLAND PUBLISHING, INC.
NEW YORK & LONDON
1985

For a complete list of the titles in this series
see the final pages of this volume.

This facsimile has been made from a copy
in the Yale University Library.

Library of Congress Cataloging in Publication Data

Eldridge, F. R.
Advertising and selling abroad.
(History of advertising)
Reprint. Originally published: New York : Harper & Brothers, 1930.
1. Advertising. 2. Export marketing. I. Title. II. Series.
HF5827.E6 1985 659.1 84-46063
ISBN 0-8240-6757-6 (alk. paper)

Design by Donna Montalbano

The volumes in this series are printed on
acid-free, 250-year-life paper.

Printed in the United States of America

ADVERTISING AND SELLING ABROAD

ADVERTISING AND SELLING ABROAD

By

F. R. ELDRIDGE

Executive Vice President, American Manufacturers Export Association
Author of "Trading with Asia," "Oriental Trade Methods," and "Financing Export Shipments"

HARPER & BROTHERS PUBLISHERS
NEW YORK AND LONDON
1930

ADVERTISING AND SELLING ABROAD

First Edition
K-E

CONTENTS

PREFACE

We are familiar with that philosophy which professes a belief in universal selling appeal and selling method. It holds that the human emotions are the same the world over and that a good can-opener will appeal to everyone everywhere. The native of Ethiopia will be intrigued by it just as effectively as will the skeptical housewife of Iowa. This philosophy proclaims, in effect, that the chief effort of the manufacturer should be concentrated in making a better article more cheaply than anyone else. He should do this either by reducing overhead through mass production or increasing production through highly paid workmen efficiently operating labor-saving machinery. With this objective of the producer we are in thorough accord.

We do not subscribe to the corollary so often expressed, however, that with such a product, selling abroad is a routine matter. Sales depots conveniently situated and attractively displaying standard products are not all that is necessary to induce people everywhere to buy. If such were the case the chain store would long since have encircled the globe.

In many places in the world, selling is still a matter of creating desires for things which we in the United States have long since adopted as routine. In too many places it is not a question of convenience or time saving that constitutes a selling appeal. Nearly half the population of the earth is still living so near to starvation that such an appeal cannot possibly move them.

A study of their actual living conditions and an adaptation of the selling appeal to their real economic status is therefore essential. Coupled with this a study of existing local methods of distribution abroad and the mapping out of an advertising and sales campaign suitable for each region is most necessary.

An investigation of what these conditions are and how our products may be made to appeal to people living under them, as well as the many and varied means of placing our products in the hands of consumers resident in all sorts of inaccessible and remote regions, is my excuse for devoting this study entirely to the foreign field.

With correct advertising and sales methods decided upon, the next step is financing. In *Financing Export Shipments,* the companion volume, I have set forth how shipments made abroad are paid for.

Together these two volumes outline present-day standard practice in advertising, selling, and financing. In short, they enable the student, whether he be in university or business, to grasp the principles of export merchandising.

F. R. ELDRIDGE

New York, July 15, 1930

ADVERTISING AND SELLING ABROAD

ADVERTISING AND SELLING ABROAD

CHAPTER I

Advertising and Selling Abroad

To the exporter the world must become a variegated chart of human wants. He must visualize peoples in their natural environment, limited by the special hardships which nature has imposed or enjoying the peculiar benefits of economic endowment. He must reconstruct their lives for a moment and endeavor to penetrate those barriers of ignorance or want which prevent them from fulfilling certain innate desires. He must look at their potentialities rather than their actualities and see whether in that vision he may glimpse a demand for the product which he has to sell them.

Then dismissing this vision, he must turn to the conditions as they exist and plan to arouse those desires in his potential customers which will transform them into actual customers. Having determined that their purchasing power will enable them to buy his product, he must first create a demand on the part of his consumers. This he may only do through the medium of advertising. Having created consumer demand, he must perfect a dealer organization to cater to that demand and feed that dealer organization from strategically located stocks maintained by wholesalers. He must see that these wholesalers may obtain his goods at reasonable prices and with minimum delay from jobbers, who in turn will purchase directly from him. If there is faulty preparation or organization anywhere along this channel of distribution his sales will suffer. The goods must not only be fed into this channel in proper volume, but they must reach the consumer at a fair price and in time to take advantage of the demand which advertising may create. Advertising and selling abroad, therefore, like advertising and selling at home, must represent a perfectly synchronized activity or set of activities.

A Foreign Sales Campaign.—The most common error in most foreign sales campaigns is lack of planning. Too many manufacturers are catapulted into the foreign field through incipient demand which may crop up here and there throughout the world, and without considering the problem as a whole, obtain only a scanty portion of the returns their product deserves. Others may expend more time and effort than the potential possibilities of their product in most foreign markets can ever repay them. Generally speaking there are but four ways of approaching any foreign market: through direct-by-mail selling; by means of traveling salesmen; through the appointment of resident agents abroad; and by the establishment of foreign branches. The best results may often be obtained by a combination of one or more of these methods, depending upon the characteristics of the market and the peculiarities of the product itself. Some products are only saleable in certain parts of the world. Ice skates, for example, can only be sold where there is ice, whether it be natural or artificial. The native of the tropics has no use for a stove for heating purposes, nor has the Eskimo any need for an electric fan. When the world has been surveyed from all possible angles, from the standpoint of population, of climate, of economic resources, of purchasing power, then the sales campaign may be laid out intelligently, taking into consideration the character of the product itself and how it may be distributed most effectively. Once the cost of such a sales campaign has been assessed, the money for it should be appropriated with the view to carrying it out completely. No general has ever won a battle by turning back halfway. "Be sure you're right, then go ahead."

Selling Direct to the Dealer.—Many products can be sold successfully abroad directly to dealers. The usual method of reaching the dealer is by direct-by-mail advertising. The first approach, after the important detail of obtaining trustworthy mailing lists is accomplished, is by means of the introductory letter, which should be a straightforward statement of why, in your opinion, *it would be profitable* for the dealer to handle your line. There are, of course, any variety of selling appeals by means of which you may impress this fact upon him. But the fact itself should never be lost sight of. Remember he is not interested in what John Jones thinks of your product. That is consumer appeal, but it falls flat with the dealer. He is interested, however, in *how much* John Jones has made out of your product. That appeal touches him on a tender spot. He is, moreover, not so much interested in how good your product is or how cheaply it may be sold. The dealer's discount will interest him much more. In some markets direct dealer distribution is made difficult because of the credit situation. Used to receiving long accommodation from local jobbers or wholesalers, they may not be in a position to meet less lenient terms. In other places the question of transportation or inland distribution may tend to keep the product in hands of middlemen. If you are in a position to meet any of these conditions you have a direct selling appeal to the dealer. Every dealer would like to buy direct if he could, and the easier you make direct buying for him the more likely you are to get his order. If your initial letter brings no response, send a follow-up offering some special inducement like the sole agency for a town or certain district on the basis of a stipulated initial order. This should be followed by a third and fourth appeal, if necessary. The process of attrition can be effectively carried out by mail, and the more you know about local prejudices against your product at home the better you will be able to appeal to the dealer abroad.

Enlisting the Consumer's Aid.—Sometimes a dealer's sales resistance can only be broken down by enlisting the aid of his customer, the consumer. Every distributor in the domestic market is familiar with the "Ask your dealer" method of direct-to-the-consumer appeal, designed primarily for the purpose of forcing the dealer to pay some attention to your product. This can be used just as effectively abroad. Many a direct-by-mail dealer campaign has had little or no effect until the consumer was appealed to direct. Then letters have been dug out of the files and orders placed by cable. When people want a certain product it is difficult for any dealer to resist them. Sometimes it is wise to give the dealer notice that you are starting such a campaign, sending him advance cuts of the ads that are to appear in his local papers on a date fixed far enough in the future to permit him to place at least a trial order and have the goods reach him before the campaign starts. In such a case the length of time that the advertisement will appear and the media used are all important considerations which may have a direct influence upon the dealer's decision. If you use the wrong media or the campaign is not of long enough duration, he may still decide to play a waiting game. The advice of the dealer on these points may sometimes, when asked, prove the first sign of life that he has evinced. Indeed, some dealers will not place initial orders for unknown products unless they are assured in advance of an advertising campaign to assist distribution.

The Foreign Traveler.—There are many types and species of traveling salesmen who operate entirely abroad. Some of these are manufacturer's agents covering a certain territory periodically with a limited number of lines. Others represent but one line and either cover a much larger territory or cover a smaller territory much more intensively than the salesman representing a number of lines. Still others may do no selling, but merely visit foreign agents periodically, keeping up their morale or adjusting differences and complaints. Other travelers are sent abroad to appoint or select agents or dealers and then return home to head up the export department at home. In any case the foreign emissary of the manufacturer or exporter is a much more potent factor in any sales campaign than the mere appeal by correspondence. The question for the principal to decide is whether the sales volume which can be obtained for his product abroad, either immediately or over a period of years, will warrant the outlay necessary to send a traveler abroad. This can be arrived at by scrutinizing export statistics covering the product as an indication of the potential demand for similar items of American manufacture and by delving into foreign import statistics as an indication of the total existing demand. Once the expense seems justified, the problem of picking the proper man, from the point of view both of his language equipment and of his familiarity with foreign conditions, as well as his knowledge of the product itself, is a task of no small magnitude. The right type of foreign traveler, whether his task be to sell or to choose agents, is by far the most effective method of reaching the right people. Next to a conscientious resident agent or foreign branch he can perform more effective work than a thousand letters.

Heralding the Traveler's Approach.—If you were talking to a small roomful of people you would not need a megaphone. So the approaching visit of a traveling salesman who is to choose dealers or agents can be announced most effectively by direct correspondence. A good deal of effective spade work, however, may be done, especially where the traveler has to choose a number of dealers in any one community, by advertising in trade papers known to reach the dealer. Such media are far less common abroad than in the United States, and where no satisfactory media exist, a small campaign in the local newspaper may serve the same purpose. In these advertisements there is not need to mention the fact that a representative is coming. Merely the ad. itself will arouse enough interest, as a rule, to lighten the task of the traveler considerably. His product will at least be known. It will be an advertised product and as such will become more attractive to the dealer than if he had never heard of it. Many dealers abroad subscribe to one or more trade papers in the United States and sometimes an advertisement in such media to the effect that dealers abroad are wanted will have surprising results. The people who reply to such advertisements may or may not be the type of people wanted as dealers, but their replies at least show where the market lies. Some American trade papers with a foreign dealer or jobber circulation are printed in Spanish, Portuguese, French, Italian, etc. In many countries these have attained large circulations and form excellent media for the purpose of preparing the way for the foreign traveler.

Direct and Indirect Selling.—One of the most puzzling problems for some manufacturers and exporters to decide is whether their goods can be handled to best advantage by dealers direct or through sole agents appointed to cover one or more sales territories. Of one thing there can be no doubt. No combination of the two systems has been known to work satisfactorily. The real test as to which method of distribution should be chosen lies in the character of the goods themselves. Generally the same type of goods which may be successfully distributed in this country through dealers may be handled in the same way abroad. Standard products carrying their own selling appeal for which there is a steady demand may generally be successfully distributed directly through dealers abroad, provided sufficient consumer demand is created for your particular product to retain the dealers' interest. On the other hand, products which require a considerable amount of selling effort, or which, because of their character, are unfamiliar to the buying public of any given foreign country, require the special effort of a resident agent, who, because of the introductory effort which he must put into the line, will want it on a sole-agency basis for a definite period of years. A most common mistake, and a fatal one, is to appoint a dealer as sole agent for a whole country or large sales area. His competitors will not buy from him if they can possibly avoid it. His initial order may be attractive and he may even agree to purchase a fair amount each year, but no matter what promises he makes, the manufacturer can rest assured that he will not get other dealers to buy from him. A resident agent may get wider distribution for a product because he can sell all dealers on the same terms.

Synchronizing Advertising and Selling.—There are few standard specialty products that can be sold today in any great volume without advertising. If a product is advertised at home it certainly must be advertised abroad, and, conversely, merely because a product may attain a certain distribution at home without advertising is no criterion that it can obtain the same relative distribution abroad, without advertising. Many unadvertised products at home are chain-store items and chain stores, with the exception of one or two still in the experimental stage in England and Germany, do not exist abroad. Others are still selling on the reputations attained through intensive advertising in the past. This can be of no possible assistance abroad unless the advertising campaign happened to be a foreign as well as a domestic one. The fact is that, in addition to demanding a sole-agency agreement, most resident agents abroad will require a certain amount of advertising before they will consent to take on the agency for a standard specialty. Sometimes, like the dealers, good agents can only be interested in a product if consumer demand is created in advance. In all countries there are definitely established buying seasons. These usually occur twice a year and correspond roughly with the harvest seasons. In order to prepare for these consumer buying seasons resident agents must place indents sometimes four months in advance, depending upon their remoteness from the source of supply. The advertising campaign must be timed to extend through the consumer buying season, while the orders from dealers may be accelerated if the resident agent is reinforced in his personal canvassing by a direct-by-mail or trade-paper campaign two to four months before the buying season opens.

When Branches Pay.—The establishment of a branch selling office abroad can be determined almost entirely upon volume of sales. Branch-office expense is a fixed item and should bear a definite relation to sales volume. Resident agents working entirely on commission may build up a volume of sales that nets them a compensation far in excess of what it is estimated the establishment of a branch would cost. Many manufacturers and exporters have acted ruthlessly in throwing overboard good agents as soon as their volume has been built up, many times with disastrous results. Their branch managers, usually inexperienced in the territory, have found a certain loyalty among dealers to the old agent, and merely on the basis of this loyalty, many an ex-agent has sought and obtained a competitive line with which he has wrecked the business of his ex-principal's branch. It is usually the case that resident agents abroad have only a few "bread and butter" lines from which they earn the major portion of their income. If their dominant principal approaches them with the proposal to convert their agency into a branch, paying the agent a fixed salary with an over-riding commission and assuming all the expenses, the proposition may prove profitable to both parties. Many successful branches of progressive exporters and manufacturers abroad are today staffed with the personnel of an ex-agent. The bonus or over-riding commission is an essential feature of such an arrangement if the principal is to retain the same energetic enthusiasm on the part of his new branch manager, as was instrumental in building up the business on a commission basis.

Should Advertising be Handled Locally?—Many agents request that they be allowed a certain percentage on sales for local advertising. They argue that, being on the spot, they can get the best results by appealing to strictly local prejudices unknown to the manufacturer thousands of miles away. Too often their plea is heeded, usually with the stipulation that they furnish evidence of the expenditure of the allowance. Granted that an agent is sincere in his efforts to get the best results from such an advertising allowance, he is often hampered by a lack of experience in advertising technique. Merely because an agent is a good salesmen is no criterion of his ability as an advertising agent. Questions of lay-out, of position, and the expense of making cuts in newspaper advertising soon become inextricably confused with questions of location and type of appeal for billboards or street-car advertisements. Moreover, an agency in the United States, besides being expert in all these things, has an added advantage of having more than the advertising of one product to place in any given local medium. It is seldom that a local selling agent, even though he knows the management of a newspaper personally, can get the same rate concession that can be obtained by a large American agency which is placing thousands of inches monthly. Then comes the much mooted question of local appeal in the advertising matter itself. The champions of local advertising claim that local scenery and local types appeal much more strongly than those "made in America" and shipped to the local media in the form of wood blocks or engravings. The American agencies claim that carefully thought-out "copy" which has made a successful appeal in the United States will prove equally successful everywhere.

A Few Cases.—The most successful exporters today have traveled the same route. Beginning their exporting almost simultaneously with their domestic business, they have followed the same general principles abroad as have been the basis of their success at home. If they distribute through dealers in the United States they have done the same thing abroad, and if their line is such as can be handled most advantageously by jobbers in the United States, resident agents abroad have been found to be the proper medium. As their business has grown and they have established branches at home, the volume of their foreign business has been found to warrant the same step in many foreign countries. As with their distribution so with their advertising. Products which sell best through billboard advertising at home can usually be introduced abroad through the same medium with greatest advantage. Where newspapers are found to be the best medium at home, they are equally effective abroad. In short, these successful exporters have found that human reactions do not change with the pigment of the skin or the amount of clothes one wears. They do change, however, with climate and habitat. Generally speaking, people of the plains think alike the world over, while mountaineers have a peculiar psychology all their own whether they reside in Tibet or the Andes. Likewise, people of the tropics and semi-tropics are much alike whether they live in Sumatra or Africa. Race and environment may cause certain variations, but basically they are much the same. In this country with all types of people we have developed more or less of a universal sales appeal, and for this reason what appeals to the American generally appeals to the world.

Some Conclusions.—After you as an exporter have surveyed the world from the standpoint of the potential purchasing power of various countries as applied to your particular product, you should map out a sales campaign abroad that will fit these conditions, basing your method on the character of your commodity. If dealers are to be sold direct, let your appeal to them be based on the profits to be made from your line. Create customers for them by direct-to-consumer advertising. If your written appeal to them is without result, consider the advisability of sending a traveler abroad to appoint dealer distributors, and fortify him with sufficient publicity on your line so that the goods he seeks to place will not be entirely strange to the foreign representative. If your product requires special selling effort it may not be wise to depend upon dealer distribution. In those circumstances you should appoint a resident sole agent for each country or large sales territory, but in no case should an agent be a dealer, for you thereby forfeit the business of all his competitors. Such an agent should be backed up by substantial advertising so timed as to coincide with the buying seasons, whenever they might occur. When the sales volume of such agents reaches a point where it becames profitable to consider opening a branch, do not ignore the agent who has helped you build up your business. Good agents are not necessarily experts in the art of advertising and their wishes in the matter of placing advertising locally should not always be complied with. Finally, it is wise to follow the same method of distribution and advertising abroad as has been found successful at home, unless peculiar local circumstances dictate a deviation in some instances.

CHAPTER II

Formulating a Foreign Sales Campaign

Many exporters today are neglecting potential markets for their products merely because they have not taken the trouble to investigate these markets, and no one else has thought of suggesting it to them. A manufacturer will receive an inquiry from abroad. It may be the first inquiry for his goods that he has ever received. Instead of reasoning that if one dealer or one agent in that market is interested in handling his product, many other dealers and agents must be interested, he will accept the first proposition that is made to him. Merely in order to sell a bill of goods he will often tie up valuable territory under a long-term sole-agency contract with an agent or dealer whose outlets and facilities in no way warrant the gratuity. It will, perhaps, never occur to him that foreign markets, like home markets, can easily be accorded sales quotas, that the same principles apply to granting an agency for the state of Arizona as apply to the granting of a sales agency for the whole of Brazil. Cases are actually on record where manufacturers have built up a splendid domestic business by the application of sound sales principles and have violated every one of these principles when the question of apportioning foreign sales territory came to be considered.

Considering the Foreign Market as a Whole.—There is a wealth of data available on all of the factors which must be considered prior to the sound formulation of a foreign sales campaign. The Department of Commerce alone publishes at nominal cost authentic reports which supply a wealth of background information upon which a sales campaign abroad for almost any commodity may be built. Some of the questions which must be answered in any survey of this character are of a fundamental character. What is the population? How is it distributed? Upon what export products does it depend for the funds with which to purchase foreign products? What products are now in greatest demand? From what countries are they purchased? Do the sales abroad exceed the purchases from abroad? If not, what "invisible" items—i.e., services, remittances from abroad, tourists' expenditures in the country, etc.—help the population to pay for the excess of imports? Is the volume of foreign purchases and sales increasing?

All of these questions may be answered from three annual publications of the Department of Commerce: *The Commerce and Navigation of the United States,* the *Statistical Abstract,* and the *Commerce Yearbook.* If more detailed information is required as to the trend and volume of domestic business within a given foreign country, the unpublished material in the files of the Department of Commerce at Washington and the yearbooks and returns of trade of the various countries on file there will furnish this information also. It is not necessary to go to Washington to get such information, however, for the large libraries of all the principal cities are fully equipped to serve the public in such matters.

Determining How to Sell.—After the market has been measured, after the exporter is assured that considerable numbers of people throughout the world do use or could use his product, the most important step is to determine how the product can be placed where they can buy it. It can be assumed that the retailer or dealer abroad is the logical outlet for most lines of merchandise. This does not mean, however, that retailers in all countries are equipped to handle imports from abroad. As a matter of fact, most of them are not. They are merchants of small capital who are not especially good credit risks and are in many instances as ignorant of the United States and our ways of doing business as we are of them. Many of them, however, if approached by a salesman speaking their own language and offered goods from abroad by sample with prices quoted c. i. f. the nearest port, or better still, delivered prices at their warehouses, will consider direct importation or "indenting," provided they do not have to tie up their capital to do so. Very few of these dealers will pay any attention to letters from manufacturers unless they are reinforced by a personal call. The traveling salesman, therefore, in most instances, is a necessary adjunct to a dealer campaign. Not only is he often necessary in the proper selection of dealers, but his actual presence once or twice a year, at the order-taking season, is highly desirable and in most cases absolutely essential. Often more effective than the occasional traveler is the resident agent who handles no stock but is in constant touch with the dealer and accepts his orders, which are forwarded to the manufacturer for direct shipment to the dealer. Such an agent also sees that the dealer pays the drafts drawn on him by the manufacturer. The agent who is willing to guarantee payment or accept drafts, more often acts in the capacity of a full-fledged jobber, buying outright what his trade wants and charging an advance over the manufacturers' prices for his handling of the financial end. Such jobbers, instead of representing a group of manufacturers as the manufacturers' agent does, often has a buying representative in New York who shops around for him and buys on commission. Obviously a manufacturer who sells abroad in this manner is not exporting. He is merely providing a foreign importer with goods. The direct representative of the manufacturer in a foreign market, residing there year in and year out and carrying some stocks for immediate dealer requirements, is undoubtedly the most effective method of foreign merchandising. Such a method, except on a large volume, is expensive, and can, therefore, seldom be made to pay, especially at the beginning. The first task of the exporter is to determine which of these methods of distribution is best suited to his peculiar needs.

Salesman and Dealer.—Goods which are staples, change little in style, and are not subject to wide price fluctuation will often be stocked by jobbers, wholesalers, or retailers abroad, as the interest on the investment is often smaller than the loss sustained by shortage of stocks in the face of a growing demand. The more remote the markets from the factory, the greater is the tendency to carry at least three months' supply of goods. In most of our important but remote markets, therefore, such as Argentina, Brazil, and Chile, South Africa, India, China, Japan, the Philippines, and Dutch East Indies, Malaysia and Australasia, the tendency is to buy from twice to four times a year. This tendency is further accentuated by the fact that most of these markets are great agricultural countries with two crops, one harvested in the spring and the other in the fall. The merchants accordingly wish to be fully stocked up when the money from these crops is most readily available. They, therefore, place their orders about four months before these peaks of demand or around the 1st of December and the 1st of June. This is usually the time for the salesman who is traveling abroad to plan to reach these markets, as the channels of distribution are then most receptive. It will be noticed that the markets mentioned, however, are situated at long distances from each other. It is a month's journey from Buenos Aires to Johannesburg even if good connections are made; from South Africa to India requires at least three weeks, and from India to China another two weeks. It is a physical impossibility for a single traveler to cover all of the principal markets twice a year. The best any man could do would be to cover these markets once a year and then only by skillful planning would he arrive in each place even approximately during the buying season. A sales campaign must either be planned to cover a single trade area like South America or at least three or four travelers must be provided to cover each territory effectively and at the right time. It is well to remember that salesmen from all other exporting countries will be flocking to these markets at approximately the same time. The dealer, wholesaler, or jobber will buy what is offered at the right time and the right price. The attempt to get direct and wide distribution through primary distribution agencies abroad, unless attempted on a big scale, had better be confined to restricted areas. All of this must be considered when planning the campaign so that those areas may be chosen which represent the greatest potential markets for the manufacturer's product.

Traveler and Agent.—Where style changes are a ruling factor or where price fluctuation makes the quick turnover of goods essential, it is often difficult to get either jobber, wholesaler, or dealer abroad to stock goods in any great quantity. As a rule orders are placed on a monthly or fortnightly basis, and the distributor arranges his purchases so that small lots of goods are constantly arriving and he is enabled to take advantage of changes in either design or price. A resident agent to handle such business is almost essential. The traveling representative of the manufacturer, however, can perform a most useful service in periodic visits to these agents, checking up on their activities, calling on customers, adjusting complaints, and in other ways injecting a certain *esprit de corps* into a sales organization which might otherwise easily become out of touch with the factory. If such a line-up is decided upon, the traveler should be carefully selected. He should preferably be more than a factory representative. While thoroughly conversant with the problems of production, he should be familiar with at least the principal languages of the territory he is to cover—if Latin America, Spanish; or if Europe, French and German, and also Spanish and possibly Italian. He should be above all a diplomat, able to adjust himself to local conditions and to adapt the company's policies to such conditions as he meets. The agents he selects will look upon him as the company's representative and he must always attempt to live up to the rôle. Whatever he does in an agent's territory will reflect not only upon the agent's business, but upon the company's product. It is better to send no one abroad at all than the wrong man.

Selection of Markets.—If a world-wide campaign is deemed inexpedient at the start, the next most important step, after determining the type of representative, is to select the markets. In order to do this effectively, a considerable amount of background information is necessary. Often where the product is new, there is little or nothing in trade returns to indicate where the larger demand is. If it is machinery of certain types, the problem of determining the places in the world where industries of the type exist is relatively simple. Some products are in almost universal use, such as clocks, fire-extinguishers, etc., while other things, such as the classical ice skate, have distinct geographical limitations. Some markets, such as Australia, New Zealand, and South Africa, use practically everything that is used in the United States, while others, such as India and China, are restricted by local custom which render some of the most commonly used American articles unsaleable. Out of this welter of conflicting habits—dress, living conditions, customs and religious and social prejudices—the exporter must select the best markets in which to give his goods a try-out. There is no royal road by which a knowledge of these things can be reached. The export advertising agencies may prove helpful, the Department of Commerce, through its commodity divisions, can certainly supply a great deal of useful information. The selection and application of general information to a particular problem is a thing that can probably be done better by the manufacturer or export manager himself, especially if he has traveled and observed conditions at first hand.

Effects of Immature Planning.—Many a manufacturer is struggling along with his "export problems" today, getting little return from his efforts abroad merely because he has never stopped to analyze his selling plan and does not realize that the fault lies not in his goods or prices, but in the *type* of foreign representation he has chosen. It is just as likely that he is making a mistake in selling through an export commission house when he should have agents of his own abroad, as that he is scattering his ammunition over too wide a territory by circularizing dealers when his product could possibly be handled to better advantage by a combination export manager or manufacturers' agent. There are definite reasons why each method of distribution exists. It is the manufacturer's duty to determine what these reasons are and apply them to his own individual case. Not long ago in the course of a casual conversation with a manufacturer, he expressed his utter lack of faith in exporting.

"I can't understand how some of these fellows," he remarked, referring to the speakers at the convention we were attending, "get any business abroad at all. My export department has been in the red for four years, and I'm about to give it up."

Further questioning developed the fact that although he distributed his product at home through sole distributors in domestic sales territory, he had no real plan abroad. He mentioned his agent in one country, India, as being a well-known firm whom I recognized as a department store. I asked him if any of his domestic distributors were department stores. He indignantly denied any such lack of business acumen. Our conversation opened his eyes. He has built up his export outlets on the principle of "first come first served" instead of intelligently studying the agency arrangements in each market.

"Out of the Frying Pan into the Fire."—On another occasion a manufacturer came to me for the names of export commission houses. I had run across his product in several foreign markets, but never in the dealers' showcases where it belonged. On the other hand, I had encountered it in hardware stores, although it was a quick-selling household specialty which belonged in drug stores and department stores. I asked him why he was giving up his present method of distribution.

"Oh, I'm tired of wasting money on advertising. I even raised my agents' commission to 15 per cent, but it's no use. I'm through. If I can get a good export commission house to pay me in New York I figure I can make money on half the volume."

Then I explained to him that there were "agents and agents" abroad, and that while some were organized to sell hardware, these were not necessarily the most suitable outlets for his particular product. In order to prove it to him I suggested the names of one or two foreign agents who, in the markets with which I was familiar, should prove more effective, and told him why.

A month or two later he came to me for more names of the same type. All thought of being "through" had left him. He had merely just begun to see the possibilities for his product under proper representation. Moreover, by advancing his dealers' commissions and reducing his agents' commissions he had placed the emphasis where it belonged in his particular sales set-up.

Building Rome In a Day.—It is a common occurrence in this day of hectic sales victories at home to encounter a manufacturer who intends to "tell the cock-eyed world" all about it. His enthusiasm, unless stemmed in time, sometimes brings queer consequences. This situation is particularly true of drug and pharmaceutical products.

I once ran across the advertisement of one of these products in an Indian periodical. It pleaded with the Hindu who took his daily bath in a pool covered with green slime to spray his throat before entering crowds. The advertisement intrigued me. I called on the distributors, a Parsi merchant in Bombay. Did he sell much of the product? Yes, it was going very well. I was nonplused. India is full of surprises, but I thought I knew my India better than that. "Ah yes, sahib, all the Eurasian girls buy it." "Eurasian girls!" I gasped. The plot was thickening. "Oh yes. Three or four applications and the skin turns three shades whiter!"

Nothing, I suppose, under the circumstances, could convince this manufacturer that the Hindu is not a highly sanitary person.

Notwithstanding these few phenomenal successes in the face of all experience, the policy of "making haste slowly" is usually the best. The Chinese were induced to eat raisins only after painstaking investigation developed the fact that the five-cent packages were being split up and sold at one copper cash for a dozen or so raisins. Now China is flooded with small paper envelopes of raisins that sell at the unit of value most common among the Chinese. The Singer Sewing Machine Co. first taught the women of China to sew by machine, just as the Standard Oil Co. taught them to discard the vegetable-oil-tallow wicks and use kerosene lamps. The other day I read of a shipload of American fresh fruit leaving for Oriental ports, where, ten years ago, due to lack of proper refrigeration, it was impossible to buy them at any price.

Coals to Newcastle.—Sooner or later every manufacturer who attempts to export is amazed to find that the reason he cannot sell his product in some particular market is because it has an article more suited to its needs "right in its own back yard." Purveyors of soft drinks in the Argentine find it hard to compete with "yerbe matte," a native brew that carries with it a tradition. It is popularly believed that the *gaucho* draws his tremendous vitality from his early morning "matte," which he sucks through a metal "straw." The Japanese patent-medicine manufacturer has cleverly capitalized the Chinese belief in the invigorating properties of "ginseng." "Ginseng" is the peculiar man-shaped root of a plant grown in China, Korea, and in some of our northwestern states. So far as any one has been able to discover, it has no medicinal properties whatever, but the Chinese believe that by eating it they will have sons to worship at the family shrine—a most desirable eventuality in China. Playing on this belief, the Japanese have manufactured small brown pills, equally free of all real medicinal value, and have sold them by the millions under the name of "jintan." As a trade name this is a winner, for while "ginseng" merely means "man-like form," "jin-tan" means "man-like vigor." Even coals can be sold in Newcastle if they are properly advertised!

"Be Sure You're Right, Then Go Ahead."—Unless a sales campaign is properly planned abroad, much time and money can be lost. Once the elementary studies have convinced the manufacturer, however, that a market exists for his product, nothing should deter him from following up an intelligent campaign. It is often disheartening to spend thousands of dollars in advertising without seeing any return. It is equally disheartening to select distributors abroad only to find that for some months their efforts seem to meet with no response. Too many manufacturers, however, become discouraged before they have given the market a fair trial. It takes time to educate a people, not only to a new product, but to an entirely new method of living, which in many cases develops from the use of a new product. The gradual conviction, only now growing upon the people of India, that hookworm is an infection of the foot which can be eradicated by the wearing of shoes, has created a market for millions of pairs of shoes among a people who had formerly gone barefoot. The idea that lights at night attract insects has developed a tremendous demand for flashlights throughout the tropics, where screening is too expensive for the average native abode. In both instances the idea was right, although its adoption for a long time seemed hopeless. Now the manufacturers who stuck by their guns are reaping the harvest.

CHAPTER III

PLANNING A FOREIGN ADVERTISING CAMPAIGN

AMERICAN products selling abroad, aside from the great staple commodities, are all of a character that require extensive advertising. To foreigners America is the land of Yankee ingenuity. To them it seems that everything in America must have by this time become automatic. From our motion pictures they have conceived the positive conviction that ALL Americans ride about in motor-cars practically all the time; live in palatial residences presided over by obsequious butlers and chic French maids; spend what time can be snatched from golf to cruise around in yachts and otherwise enjoy, as common individuals, the pastimes and privileges typical only of the lives of royalty and millionaires in their own country. Naturally they aspire to become like us.

To the European today the word "American," when prefixed to a product as a descriptive adjective, immediately brings up the same mental picture that "imported" or "direct from Paris" conjures up in our own minds. They are intrigued, especially if the article is something that has never been used or heard of. They will buy it if the price is within their reach and especially if it takes the place of something in everyday use that does not carry all the glamour of the "American" product. Two of the principal selling arguments, therefore, of most American products abroad are that they are NEW and that they are CHEAP AT THE PRICE.

American Advertising Methods Successful.—Motor-car manufacturers were the first to discover that American advertising methods are just as successful abroad as they are at home. Before their entrance into the advertising field abroad there were innumerable space brokers who had called themselves "export advertising agencies," but whose principal function was to line up as many foreign publications as they could, bargaining for the outright control of all the space sold to American advertisers. They, at least, furnished the American advertiser reasonable assurance that the funds appropriated were actually spent for space in foreign media as they presented vouchers with their invoices. They did not provide, however, because of the very nature of their operations, any opportunity for an intelligent selection of media for efficient market coverage. As competition between American manufacturers in the foreign market increased, the more progressive of these brokers began to realize the necessity of giving better service to advertisers, with the result that they endeavored to gain an actual knowledge of foreign market conditions so that they could plan campaigns covering all media, not especially those whose space they controlled, and write copy as well as design advertisements that would "pull" abroad just as domestic agencies had been doing in the home market for a

HAD IK MAAR DADELIJK EEN HOOVER AANGESCHAFT

Is een verzuchting, die menige huisvrouw slaakt, als haar het verschil wordt aangetoond tusschen den Hoover en een gewonen stofzuiger. Geen wonder, de prestaties van den Hoover overtreffen verre die van welken anderen stofzuiger ook. De Hoover toch is de eenige machine, die door zijn „Positieve Agitatie" Uw kleeden klopt, het vuil opveegt en direct in den stofzak zuigt. Daardoor wordt het diepst ingezakte vuil, het zand, dat Uw kleeden vernielt, grondig verwijderd.

Gaarne willen wij U op Uw eigen kleed een demonstratie geven en U inlichten over den inruil van Uw verouderde machine en onze zeer gemakkelijke betalingsvoorwaarden die neerkomen op slechts 38 cents per dag.

N.V. DE HOOVER-HANDELMAATSCHAPPIJ
Het Hooverhuis
Falckstraat 15-29, Amsterdam Telefoon 36251 & 36271

De nieuwe HOOVER

Ged. Merk

KLOPVEEGZUIGER

Hij KLOPT . . . en hij Veegt . . . en hij Zuigt

COPY THAT "PULLS" AT HOME WILL "PULL" ABROAD

number of years. The advent of the real export advertising agency operating much as it does today was the next step. That the projection of these domestic methods into the foreign markets of the world has been an unqualified success is no longer disputed, even though, in the most successful agencies, the necessity of adherence to the foreign or local taste in many particulars is admitted and carefully provided for.

Types of Export Advertising Method—"Centralized Control."—The most successful agencies in the field today are those who have applied American methods of merchandising and advertising THROUGH organizations abroad which provide the machinery for local operation and the assembling of market knowledge. In working out such a dual system, emphasis is placed first on the personal contact maintained with the manufacturer in America, where centralized control over every phase of advertising policy, selection of media, and creation of advertisements is maintained. Secondly on the personal contact, through the affiliated or branch advertising agency abroad, with the manufacturer's distributor or dealers in the market where the advertising is actually applied. This is known as the "centralized control" method and its advantages are many. The manufacturer knows in advance exactly what is planned for each market. He approves every move before it is made and has positive proof that his wishes are being carried out. Estimates of all costs are submitted for advance approval and every bill from the agency is supported by a voucher copy of the advertisement as it has appeared in the foreign media. There is no guess as to what is being done or how the budget is actually being spent. From this point agency practice varies.

The foreign associated agency in one case furnishes, direct from the scene of the selling operation, data upon which the advertisements are based and the campaign planned. The "copy," after it has been created by the home agency and approved by the manufacturer, is sent abroad to be checked by the foreign associate agency before it is "proofed" for insertion. The proofs of the advertisement before its appearance are shown to either the manufacturer's dealer or representative as a final precaution. The space-buying is done abroad locally to assure the lowest rate and to take advantage of the foreign associate agency's better knowledge of media and their drawing power and reader influence. In other cases this work is handled directly with the foreign newspapers from the home agency, with less satisfactory results.

"Decentralized Control" Method.—Under the alternate method of decentralized control the manufacturer sends his appropriation for an export advertising campaign abroad to be handled either by his branches, if he has any, or by his agents or dealers. In only about 5 per cent of the business handled in this manner does an agency ever exercise any control over the disbursements. All plans and work in connection with the advertising, such as selection of media, space-buying, writing of copy, art-work purchase, making of engravings, approval of complete advertisements, checking of the actual appearance of advertisements, payment of invoices, are taken care of by the local sales representative. The manufacturer either sends him a lump sum or, more often, arranges for a certain percentage on sales to be deducted from his invoices for the goods distributed. Mechanical costs under this method are necessarily high, due to the duplication in art work and set-up of advertisements. No manufacturer at home permits his domestic sales representatives to handle his domestic advertising to any large degree. The fact that a foreign branch or dealer has made a success at selling is no proof that it or he know advertising. Many manufacturers have discovered this to their sorrow. Much money cheerfully appropriated by the manufacturer for foreign advertising in this manner has been wasted or actually misappropriated. Many experienced exporters, therefore, who have run the gamut of such experiences in the world's markets, have turned to the American advertising agency, with adequate representation abroad, as the producers of the most effective results.

The Work of the American Agency Under Centralized Control.—The American agency, cooperating closely with the manufacturer, plans the world-wide advertising campaign. Appropriations are set up for each market based on such factors as population, purchasing power, per-capita purchasing power, etc. Foreign media are selected on the basis of circulation, reader influence, territory covered, etc., from reliable records furnished by the foreign associated agencies. Schedules are devised for each medium and estimates accurately worked out to form the basis for individual budgets for each market. The actual advertisements are next created in the American office of the agency. These are put into portfolio form and sent to the associate agencies and to the foreign distributors. The associate agencies are given rigid instructions. Budgets must not be exceeded without the approval of the home office. Media may be varied only with its permission. Schedules for appearances are subject to readjustment by the distributors. Where associate agencies exist translations and advance proofs of all advertisements may have the approval of the distributors before they can be run. All drawings of the product for general advertisements are made in America. Cuts, electrotypes and mats of illustrations and complete advertisements are made in America. The elimination of duplication in this art work is a real economy. However, the more important factor in centralized control of art work is the uniformity of advertising that is gained. There will, under this method, be no inferior presentation of the product in any country, no matter how poor the facilities for art work. Direct-mail campaigns are handled in much the same way as press advertisments. The American agency creates the campaign and issues a portfolio of instructions. The local distributor selects and approves one or more of these creations for local application. The associate agency carries out the mechanical work of letting the printing job and selecting the mailing lists. If conditions permit, the printing is done in America, the home agency supplying all translations, reading proof and taking care of all details.

Work of the Associate Agency Abroad.—The associate agency abroad is presumably familiar with, and well informed on local conditions. This is not true in all cases, however, and the best of them will operate only as intelligently as they are instructed to do. They consult freely with the local sales agency to learn the peculiarities of the American product and the selling angles to be stressed. They obtain all necessary market data which are forwarded to the American agency for the purpose of compiling budgets and mapping out the advertising campaign. They obtain from the foreign distributor an accurate picture of what he wishes to accomplish, based upon his experience and selling problems. His views on suitable media are obtained. If the associate agency concurs in his views, they are forwarded to the American agency with approval. Otherwise the reasons for disapproval are forwarded. When the complete world-wide campaign has been built in America and the advertisements, budgets, and schedules approved by the manufacturer and put in portfolio form, they are forwarded to the associate agency. The portfolio invariably contains more advertisements than are needed by any single sales area. The distributor thus has an opportunity to select such of the advertisements as he likes.

If special conditions or occasions warrant, he may even create any special advertisement or campaign. The associate agency translates the advertisements into the native language. He attends to all details such as orders to publications, shipments of electrotypes or matrices. While schedule of insertion dates may be revised by agreement between distributor and associate agency, the total number of advertisements can only be charged in accordance with a formula safe-guarding against any exceeding of the space appropriation. If special conditions, such as increase in business or unusual opportunities, present themselves, the matter is presented through the American agency to the manufacturer for approval. The necessity for strong guidance and control is always present.

Supplementary Activities of Agencies.—Analysis of existing market data, personal researches in the foreign market, and special market investigations are all supplementary activities of foreign advertisement agencies as they are of domestic agencies. Many agencies will prepare detailed plans for the procedure necessary to start operations in a given foreign market. The customs of the native trade and the dealer outlets are all fully described and definite recommendations are made as to how to proceed. Sales quotas and sales records, arranged according to countries, trading areas, and by seasons are furnished according to the individual needs of each client. Merchandising policies and possible sales channels are suggested. Names of suitable distributors and dealers are supplied with accurate reports on the names suggested. The personal contact of the associate agencies abroad enables the agency to stimulate the enthusiasm of the distributors. Special local campaigns may often be arranged with the dealers or distributors to further the sales of the client's products and tie-in with the major advertising effort. By means of mailed questionnaires to the associate agencies abroad, important research work on the question of handling individual products in a given foreign market is often undertaken. Through the same medium a private check-up on the effectiveness of existing sales outlets of a manufacturer may be undertaken, conducted in such a way as not to disturb the existing arrangements.

Space-Buying Through Agencies.—There are no publishers' associations abroad which standardize rates, agency commissions, and discounts, with the result that *caveat emptor* is the universal rule. The question of how the various concessions from the published rates of the foreign media can be fully appropriated by the American advertiser is always a most important one. A few foreign publications of lesser importance allow as high as 30 per cent to 40 per cent commissions to agencies who bring them business but the practice is looked upon with disfavor by the leading advertising agencies. In addition there are space and time discounts depending upon the volume of space and the number of times the ad is run. The average discount allowed by the leading publications is 10 per cent to 20 per cent. Most reputable American agencies now pass on to their clients the benefits of all agency commissions, space and time discounts, and special concessions of this sort and add a service charge on the net. On all space estimates one agency I know of shows the card rate of the foreign publication, the commission or discount allowed to it and either deducts from or adds to the basic rate a percentage which establishes for it a 15 to 20 per cent gross commission depending on the budget. This is the accepted income of domestic advertising agencies. Other export agency charges range from 15 per cent net to 20 per cent gross. Much depends upon the individual space-buying ability of an agency. They must have accurate data on media values, coverage, and circulation, reader influence, etc. A reliable agency can usually save more than the commission paid it by the efficient and expert handling of such details.

Terms and Billing.—The policy of most agencies on charges and billing is comparatively simple. They bill at net prices on all work that they must buy outside their own organization, such as drawings, engravings, electrotypes, etc. To this they add a service charge of 15 per cent. On supplementary advertising copy produced through themselves, they add a service charge of 15 per cent to cost of printing and other mechanical charges. The printing and mechanical work may be handled by the client, in which case they charge only for writing copy, adding a 15 per cent service charge to net cost. In every case where expense to the client is involved they furnish, as a rule, an estimate in advance for approval. All invoices for mechanical charges are accompanied by proofs of the work plus the invoices they have paid in the client's interest. Usually, bills to the client are payable fifteen days after the date of the New York invoice. Most agencies bill twice a month, on the 15th and 30th. In normal cases when a foreign associate agency pays in August for work done or space used in July, the New York agency will receive the invoice about the 20th of September, crediting the associate in the second half of September. They will send the client an invoice dated September 30th, due October 15th. Space used in July abroad, therefore, would not be paid for by the advertiser in America until approximately ninety days later.

Domestic Agencies With Foreign Branches.—The type of foreign advertising agency described above is engaged solely in export advertising. Many domestic agencies are now actively engaged in export advertising. Some of them have opened up foreign branches, while others operate through associate agencies. Some manufacturers leave to such domestic agencies the question of apportioning the appropriation between foreign and domestic advertising, in most instances using sales volume as a basis.

Publishers' Representatives.—Many foreign publications have publishers' representatives in New York who solicit advertising direct from manufacturers. These do not attempt to perform any of the functions of an export advertising agency. Such representatives deal direct with the domestic agencies, especially those with inadequate foreign representation.

Three Methods of Approach.—In soliciting a new account an export advertising agency may make his approach in one of three ways. The minimum budget basis may be the avenue of approach. This means that the agency agrees to handle the account only on condition that the total budget for export advertising is not smaller than a given minimum. This is usually based upon the overhead expenses of the agency, and indicates the minimum basis on which the agency can afford to operate. Much depends, of course, upon the present volume of the agency's business as to the minimum budget they will accept. Other agencies will accept any account merely for the purpose of earning the commission, placing service second. Still others will undertake to find out for the manufacturer how much a budget is really needed to handle the demands of the foreign markets for his products. They will often undertake to do this independently of whether or not he agrees to contract with them subsequently for the agency.

How to Evaluate Agencies.—The exporter who has decided that his product requires foreign advertising would do well to write to all of the foreign agencies, as well as the domestic agencies with export advertising departments, asking them to call and discuss his problems. If his business is such as to warrant, say, only a $5,000 annual budget and only a few are interested, he may have them outline to him how they propose to handle his foreign advertising. If his budget is larger he will have a larger group of agencies willing to serve him. The contract which is finally drawn up should provide for all of the service outlined above and the commission should seldom exceed 20 per cent of the budget. Independent checking through the Bureau of Foreign and Domestic Commerce and other disinterested organizations will prevent abuses growing out of inadequate representation in given important markets, and a consequent omission of such fields from service. The Bureau can also furnish fairly up-to-date foreign media lists. Independent reports from the Bureau on the standing and effectiveness of the associate agencies abroad may prove of value. If the export advertising agency is used to select foreign distributors, their suggestions can often be checked very effectively through the records of the Commercial Intelligence Division of the Bureau in Washington or through the other recognized sources of foreign credit information. All export advertising agencies are not equally effective in all markets. Some manufacturers use one agency in one part of the world and another elsewhere, although no agency can do its best work under such circumstances. The disadvantages seem far to outweigh the advantages. In the case of many products it is essential that a large proportion of sales be spent in advertising. The selection of an export advertising agency is equally as important as the selection of an export representative or export manager.

CHAPTER IV

Reaching the Foreign Dealer

The character of the commodity determines the method of distribution. The things which a dealer abroad will buy from a catalogue are usually the goods for which there is a steady and inherent demand. The dealer knows but one master—the consumer. The amount of selling effort exerted by the average dealer at home is a fairly accurate measure of the effort which a dealer abroad will put behind any given article. If customers demand it steadily, the dealer will make every effort to obtain it. Substitution, however, is usually practiced abroad much more effectively than it is at home. With customers in the chief manufacturing countries intrenched behind protective tariff walls, the foreign product is naturally at a disadvantage.

It can be generally assumed that the products from abroad, under such circumstances, are either bought because of the quality appeal, or because the domestic industry has not developed sufficiently to permit production on a scale to warrant protection. In neutral markets, however, or in those markets where raw materials are produced and exchanged for manufactured goods from abroad, the competition is between the manufacturers of the world for such trade as exists. Despite all that has been written on the subject, the element of national antipathies plays a small part in selections of the consumer. In neutral markets, therefore, dealers think first of price, secondly of potential volume, thirdly of profit on sales, and last of all of quality. This train of thought is induced in all instances by the expressed desires of the consumer. In choosing between a German and an American portable phonograph, for example, dealers upon whom I called in India were attracted immediately by the price of the American product, which was 25 per cent below that of any other make. They calculated that with a phonograph so priced they could appeal to a whole group of persons who could not afford to buy the other makes. The dealers' discount on the American phonograph was the same as on the German. However, the American phonograph was designed for quiet summer bungalows in the Adirondacks and not for the noisy native quarter of Bombay. It was meant to croon forth the appealing sonnets of a Rudy Vallee which charmed the American flapper lolling back in her canoe, but when the screeching lilt of a Nautch dance emanated from it, the street noises of Bombay won. The German instrument screamed in just the right crescendo.

Profits Are Made On Sales.—No matter how much we had increased the dealer's commission, under such circumstances, we could not have induced him to stock the product because of inherent defects in its adaptation to the market. It is useless to try to sell the Indian customer on the mellow tone of a phonograph. Unless the customer wants it, appeal to the dealer is useless. All things being equal, however, that is price, quality, and potential sales volume, the most powerful appeal that can be made to the dealer is the discount. On this single point alone most dealers will show a willingness to display what salesmanship they possess on behalf of a given product. The first step in planning a direct sales campaign to dealers abroad, therefore, is to ascertain whether your price is right, whether your quality is equal to if not better than the product of your competitors, and whether the potential sales volume is great enough to interest the dealer. Some foreign markets are essentially price markets. The populations have such low purchasing power that it is not a question of whether they can afford a good product, but whether they can afford to purchase it at all. They will invariably buy the cheapest article if they buy at all.

Dealers' profits are made on actual sales. Unless the product will sell, he is not interested in it, no matter what discounts are offered him. Other markets are essentially quality markets. The populations have a high per capita purchasing power. Such markets are, in addition to the United States, Canada, Australia, New Zealand, Great Britain, Sweden, Norway, and Denmark. Dealers in such markets buy on the basis of quality AT A PRICE. Their customers are highly discriminating and usually know values. Even in such markets, however, prices must be such as will attract the largest volume of sales. How to gauge the potential sales volume and scale prices to meet it without sacrificing quality is the chief problem in such markets. In both instances the maintenance of sales volume is the prime essential.

Financing the Dealer.—If price and quality are right, the available dealers in a given market may be so involved with local jobbers and wholesalers that they cannot afford to take on a line, no matter how attractive, which involves a cash outlay. Terms of payment then becomes the selling point. Usually it is not wise for the manufacturer to finance the dealer. This is the function of the local banks and generally ways can be devised, provided the banks can be shown how individual dealers, who are their customers, may buy to greater advantage. In many European countries banks guarantee their customers' accounts for a consideration. In other places banks allow

THE PRICE OF A "MOVIE" SEAT *buys an* EVERSHARP!

A slim red, blue or yellow Eversharp Pencil that you can use for a lifetime—and yours for 3/6!

But make sure it's a *genuine* Eversharp. Look for the name on the pencil and the famous Eversharp features.

The only *leads that fit.*

Don't buy leads that are not *made* for the pencil—only Eversharp leads give the service you look for in an Eversharp Pencil. Finely calibrated to 1/1000th of an inch. In seven different grades, from extra hard to extra soft. 18 to the box, 9d. And the new Commercial lead in the black cylinder. In HB and B grades only, 12 to the cylinder, 6d.

Regd. Trade Mark

PENS, DESK PENS AND PENCILS

The Wahl-Eversharp Co., Ltd.
197, Great Portland Street, W.1

A PRICE APPEAL

their customers to take goods shipped against documentary drafts and pay for them as they sell them. This is usually accomplished through the use of a trust receipt or similar document.

In certain markets, dealers of good reputation, who show satisfactory turnover, are worthy of accommodation to the extent of permitting them to accept the drafts drawn 90 or 120 days after sight and take delivery of the goods. This accommodation should never be accorded except after the most rigid investigation in each individual case. Dealers who are customers of long standing are even carried on open account by some manufacturers, settling periodically. These, however, are exceptional cases. Generally, when terms of payment becomes the issue, it is well to go slowly. Selling through correspondence is full of financial pitfalls. The burden of proof should be placed squarely upon the dealer and he should convince the manufacturer beyond a doubt that he is worthy of the accommodation he seeks.

What Can Be Sold Direct.—We have already defined the class of goods which can be most advantageously sold direct to dealers abroad as staples which change little in style and price. This covers a wide variety of products and could possibly be further broken down into definite classes of such goods. The first class or group which comes under this heading is hardware. This includes both builders' supplies and household wares. Machine tools are sometimes sold in the same way, but only the more ordinary types. Office supplies form another large category.

Kitchen utensils, such as enamel ware, glassware, and patented articles of general utility value, watches, cheap jewelry, clocks, fountain pens, flashlights, fire-extinguishers, and all that array of articles which we find in the five-and-ten-cent stores and chain drug stores throughout this country are capable of being sold directly to dealers abroad. A large category of such goods is motor accessories. Garages abroad are recognized buyers of American products of this character and good results are obtained by direct selling methods. Dealers in these lines exist in all countries even where there may be no wholesalers or jobbers. A great many of these products, it is true, are sold abroad through foreign importers or agents, but they lend themselves, perhaps better than many other products, to direct sales to dealers.

Getting Around the Middleman.—Importers, jobbers, and wholesalers abroad usually exist because of certain definite conditions which demand their services. Unless their services are required, the highly competitive nature of business in most markets will soon dispense with them. In some markets one or perhaps two conditions peculiar to that territory may render the services of the middleman necessary. If it is not credit that the middleman supplies, it may be facilities of another character. In China the difficulties of up-country distribution are wrought with so many vicissitudes and perils, both from man and nature, that direct contact between dealers in places like Chungking and New

York manufacturers is impossible. The gorges of the Yangtse vie with the bandits and likin collectors to render the actual delivery of goods a highly hazardous and expensive proposition. Once the goods are delivered the question of receiving payment is complicated by the absence of a uniform currency which even the genesis of a national banking system is unable fully to cope with. Here the middleman plays an essential and almost leading rôle.

Except for a few items where highly developed organizations like the Standard Oil Co. arrange for up-country deliveries, the foreign exporting manufacturer must sell to importers and jobbers in the great ports. Unless he is prepared to invest large sums in the building up of distributing agencies of his own, he must rely upon the middleman for ultimate distribution. Under such circumstances, selling appeals addressed to dealers located outside the accessible ports are wasted ammunition, for they could not buy direct if they wished to. In other territories conditions are not so insurmountable. With the extension of railroads into Brazil, the list of accessible dealers is steadily mounting. The same is true of Colombia, where, notwithstanding the difficulties of shipping "order notify" and consequently of drawing with documents surrendered only against payment of the draft, considerable canvassing of dealers is being carried on by American manufacturers.

Types of Dealers.—In most foreign markets there are well-defined types of dealers, just as there are in the towns and cities of the United States. Cities above 500,000 population usually have drug and pharmaceutical shops, hardware stores, "soft goods" or drygoods shops, grocery stores, furniture and house-furnishing stores, and sometimes haberdasheries, women's shops, etc. In such cities there is generally at least one and often more department stores. As the towns become smaller and the number of shops decrease in proportion the tendency is to combine one or more allied lines of trade. Thus shops handling drugs, hardware, and groceries will form one type, while those handling drygoods, haberdashery and women's wear, may form another.

In still smaller places we find the general store, just as we do in our small towns in this country. It is just as obtuse to speak of "dealers in Argentina" as it would be to speak of "dealers in the Middle West." The term would include the highly specialized shops of Buenos Aires on the one hand, grouping them with the general stores of the up-country towns, and the many types and classes of dealers in Chicago as contrasted with the prairie towns, on the other. If an article sells best in cities and towns over a certain population in the United States, it is safe to say that it will sell to the same urban class abroad.

"Bricks Without Straw."—I remember being beseiged on one occasion by manufacturers of radio receiving sets who, seeing the advertisement of a company with which I was connected, for agencies, wished us to dispose of their product in certain Far Eastern territory. It was only with the greatest difficulty that we convinced them that in most of the territory at that time there were no broadcasting stations except for code messages. Had there been broadcasting stations an excellent market for receiving sets would have immediately appeared. But in China receiving sets were then classified as contraband of war, while in India the whole idea of radio broadcasting for entertainment purposes was frowned upon because of the ease with which it might be converted into agencies for propaganda. In British Malaya, where thousands of isolated rubber planters would have made enthusiastic radio fans, there was not a single broadcasting station and the same was true of the Dutch East Indies. In the few places where broadcasting did exist, the programs were so bad that set-owners soon became disgusted. Usually phonograph records were broadcast, and if songs which pleased the natives were sent out over the ether, the white populations would be bored to tears.

It is sometimes hard to convince people in this country that all countries do not have a single language and that nowhere do 110,000,000 people exist in a single group with common customs, habits, and tastes as they do in this country. The bricks for a market edifice such as ours cannot be made without the straw of common culture.

Making It Easy to Buy.—It would be well for every manufacturer to put himself in the place of the dealer who is to receive his first catalogue. First of all, will he be able to read it? There are still people who believe, apparently, that all the world is inhabited by people who speak one of two languages—

English and Spanish. I have received beautifully designed Spanish catalogues at the American consulate in Yokohama with a letter asking that I make it available to some of the local dealers "who may not understand English." I used to turn these over to the Spanish consul who had a delightful form letter prepared for such occasions which read something to the effect that as he was the head of the Spanish-speaking community of Yokohama, he had made the catalogue available through his office to the other Spanish-speaking people, who were, unfortunately, however, only five in number. If the firm would send an English catalogue he felt sure it would be more easily understood by the Japanese, most of whom read English but few of whom read Spanish. It was safe to say that outside of Latin America, English is understood by more people in the world today than any other language.

If the dealer is able to read it, will it mean anything to him? Illustrations are most important. They are worth more than reams of explanation in writing. Then there is the question of prices. If they are f. o. b. prices they mean nothing to most dealers. He hasn't the time to figure inland freight, drayage and lighterage, ocean freight, marine insurance, etc. He wants to know what it costs him at least c. i. f. or with insurance and freight added to cost. And last but not least the terms of sale often hold a peculiar interest to most dealers. Unless these details are included most dealers will not even bother to write and ask for them. They will simply ignore your letters. Too many of your competitors are only too glad to place their wares before these dealers in such a way that buying is made easy.

Water and the Stone.—Keeping everlastingly at it, however, is good advice if the effort is intelligent. If you have reason to believe that your price is right, that your quality is attractive, and that your terms are those usually quoted in that market, you should continue your campaign with just the same vigor and vitality that you have pursued at home. Invite criticism and ask to be told why no interest is displayed. If necessary use bait to get a reply—a sample offer for return of properly filled-in blank. One enterprising manufacturer sent out a circular stating that he was willing to pay the equivalent of one dollar for every photograph of a dealer's store front that he received. He received thousands of photographs which not only opened the way for further correspondence, but gave him a good idea of the general appearance and capacity of the dealer, the type of goods in his window, the effectiveness of his display, etc. Finally, when he had sold a number of orders he used the photographs to get up an attractive booklet which proved useful in attracting further dealers.

Helping the Dealer.—Many lines of merchandise are sold as much on service as on price or quality. If, in your preliminary correspondence, you can show the foreign dealer some new ways of merchandising, you can often sell him on your service as well as on your goods. Attractive counter display dummies are always interesting talking points and should be played up in all literature. The best service of all, of course, is intelligent advertising to the consumer. Sample distribution for the purpose of creating consumer demand is often effective. Booklets and leaflets mailed direct to consumers by the dealer, with his name printed or stamped on them, are commonly used. The character of the product and the procedure found most effective in the United States are determining factors. Often the manner in which the goods are packed will prove one of the best selling points. Science has recently discovered a new cellulose substance that displaces tin in the sides of the ordinary can. Instead of the picture of a tomato, the customer sees the actual tomato itself inside the transparent container. The dealer does not have to say what the contents of his containers are. The customer sees and judges their quality by the sense of sight, whereas before he had only his imagination and often a soiled label to guide him. This is an illustration of how the manufacturer can help himself by helping the dealer, by making his wares so attractive that he who runs may read.

As the Consumer Thinks So the Dealer.—Knowing one's buying public is the most essential element in selling anywhere, but the difficulties in mastering the psychology of an entire nation of different habits, customs, and social and political background are often almost insurmountable. While such knowledge is important, it can often be overestimated. Unless there is an outstanding reason for changing the methods which have been found successful at home, the manufacturer will do well to stick to his guns and attempt to educate rather than placate, perhaps at the sacrifice of advantage gained from standardization.

While certain prejudices may be overcome in this way, there is, of course, a limit. A West Coast canner once had an entire shipment of salmon rejected by his Chinese dealer. The dealer claimed that it was not in accordance with sample. The canner said that the claim was preposterous—the goods were exactly as represented. After a lengthly correspondence it developed that in printing the labels for the shipment the salmon's tail was turned up. On the sample can the salmon's tail was turned down. Therefore, said the dealer, whereas the sample indicated that the fish were alive when packed, the turned-up tails of the salmon shipped certainly indicated that they were dead when packed. He had ordered live-packed salmon and had received dead-packed salmon. The only way out of that dilemma was to print a new set of labels. Whether or not the dealer was intelligent enough to realize the difference was beside the point. He had to sell the salmon to people who had been taught to believe that a fish with a turned-up tail was a dead fish. It was cheaper to print new labels than to attempt to educate the customers.

Pride and Prejudice.—The dealer is, at best, the representative of the consumer's prejudices rather than the manufacturer's pride. He may be sold on a line, it is true, but only to the extent that he knows it will please his customers. Otherwise he would soon find himself stocked with unsaleable merchandise. The wise manufacturer who wishes to sell abroad must study the habits of his foreign buying public and conform to them as far as possible. By so doing he will have the best chance of reaching the foreign dealer.

CHAPTER V

Creating Consumer Demand

There are said to be two effective ways of appealing to the human mind—through fear and through greed. Certainly a study of the most successful advertising copy tends to bear out this statement, although, like all generalizations, it is likely to be somewhat of an over-statement. Having pictured the foreign consumer in his native habitat, however, the problem of selling him most of the products capable of being sold abroad through advertising, resolves itself into first attracting his interest. Too many consumer advertising campaigns end right there. They succeed in attracting his interest, but they do nothing further.

It is not difficult to attract the interest of most persons, and the lower their mentality the easier the mere attracting of their interest becomes. But the lower their mentality the harder it becomes to sell them after their interest has been aroused. As the scale of intelligence rises it becomes increasingly more difficult to establish a particular appeal. To the higher intelligence, there are many other appeals than that of mere ballyhoo. All that the British American Tobacco Co. used to do in China when they wished to introduce a brand of cigarettes into a new territory was to hire a brass band and start a parade. This attracted interest and sold cigarettes—eventually, after samples had been given away by the hundred and the populace had become used to them. The mere parade, however, would merely have aroused idle curiosity. Without the samples there would have been few sales. Had the dealers in that territory not been stocked with the goods and had them on display, there would have been fewer sales even after the samples were given away. And in some instances had not cigarettes been cut in half so that they could be sold to the consumer with only a copper cash to spend, there would have been still smaller sales. The British American Tobacco Co. could have sent out the most attractive literature in the world to the Chinese cigarette dealers in those small interior towns without result. They went right out and made the people come to the dealer and ask for their goods. Today there are forty billion cigarettes sold each year in China and it is the second largest import in the country.

Trading Sorobans for Cash Registers.—Just the opposite conditions were experienced by the National Cash Register in Japan. The native abacus had been used for generations in calculating sales, and the amount of the sale was then laboriously entered into the day book by means of the brush and India-ink stone tablet. There was no check on the cash, and defalcations and peculations were common. Among the unusual methods of arousing interest in cash registers was an advertisement portraying a man with his hands over his eyes. The single legend "Blind" indicated that the man, while not actually blind, was deliberately shutting out the sight of something. The inference brought out in the text, of course, was that the person who did not own a cash register was blind to what was going on from hour to hour in his sales department. Moreover, he was blind by choice and not by necessity. This advertisement "pulled" effectively, for the offer of a booklet brought in the names of many prospects throughout the country on whom salesmen called. In this case the emphasis had to be placed on arousing the interest of a busy merchant. Afterward he could be sold by appealing to his fear of having one of his trusted employees subjected to the daily temptations of easy peculation, or his greed in trying to keep from losing money himself. The difficulty in selling him was not so great as the difficulty of arousing his interest.

The Little Leaven.—A manufacturers' representative in India found himself "stuck" with a good-sized shipment of garage tools of a certain design which he had ordered in good faith and which the dealer had subsequently refused to pay for. Instead of sacrificing the shipment at a loss he determined to try an experiment. He placed some of the tools with local dealers on consignment. Then by clever connivance he sent various individuals to inquire for and purchase the tools. They, of course, stated that they wanted those particular tools because of certain virtues which they clearly pointed out to the dealer. After each dealer had disposed of half a dozen sets of tools in this way his curiosity got the better of him. He began to experiment with the tool and found it all that his pseudo-customers had claimed. The profit was good on each sale, so the dealers began to get enthusiastic. They sold out their consignments and bought more outright, and the agent who thought the shipment a dead loss on his hands ended by cabling for a repeat order from the factory. The entire experiment involved an initial outlay of the enormous sum of sixty dollars, representing the time of six men for two weeks at five dollars a week each. The profit on the first shipment alone was three times that amount. The little leaven that leaveneth the whole was all that was needed. The dealers' interest had been aroused, albeit by a clever hoax, and the merit of the product itself did the rest.

"Buy No Other."—The negative appeal is subject to the same criticism abroad as it is at home. The time spent in tearing down something in the consumer's mind could better be spent in filling it with incentive toward positive action. Knocking the other fellow's merchandise carries as little weight in foreign markets, as a rule, as it does at home. In some countries where politeness has become a ritual, it is actually resented. The positive appeal, the appeal that gives a reason or implies a benefit to be gained, is usually the most successful.

In Tokyo a phonograph company with which I was associated erected the first electrical street sign ever erected in Japan. It depicted first the Daibutsu at Kamakura—stolid, imperturbable, the emblem of in-

. . . ON THE MUCH VEXED QUESTION OF *WHAT TO GIVE*

Next time you are racking your brains, wondering what to give—just remember that *everybody* writes!

So, something by Eversharp will solve the gift problem—whether it's a wedding present or largesse for a small nephew.

Eversharp prices are from 3/6 up to six guineas.

The only *leads that fit.*

Don't buy leads that are not *made* for the pencil—only Eversharp leads give the service you look for in an Eversharp Pencil. Finely calibrated to 1/1000th of an inch. In seven different grades, from extra hard to extra soft. 18 to the box, 9d. And the new Commercial lead in the black cylinder. In HB and B grades only. 12 to the cylinder, 6d.

EVERSHARP

Regd. Trade Mark

PENS, DESK PENS AND PENCILS

The Wahl-Eversharp Co., Ltd.
197, Great Portland Street, W.1

THE POSITIVE APPEAL IS USUALLY THE MOST SUCCESSFUL

trospection and preoccupation. As this was extinguished, new lights flashed the outline of the Daibutsu leaning over, hand to ear, listening with pleased expression to our phonograph. At first Tokyo was slightly shocked, I verily believe, but the implication was so clear that many a stroller on the Ginza, the main street, would stop and be heard to exclaim:

"Ma! Nipponophone wa omoshiroi mono da na!" ("Well! The Nipponophone (our phonograph) is an interesting thing, isn't it?") When two American companies begin to tell the foreign customer how bad the other's product is, the chances are that most of their readers will believe each one of them.

"Will You Advertise?"—One of the first questions asked the manufacturers' representative after the samples have been shown the dealer is: "How much advertising are you willing to do?" Let the answer be negative, and all of the salesmanship in the world will not avail. Foreign markets, like domestic markets, are full of "cuckoo birds"—unadvertised products which are sold on the interest and appeal worked up by advertised products. Some of these have been known to supplant advertised products where the demand was thought to be so secure that nothing could affect it. In most instances the substitute has used some design, package, or slogan so nearly like the better-known make that it has simply fooled the customer. Even so, unless the quality is equal to that on which the reputation of the advertised product has been built the new-found popularity will soon wane.

There is nothing like advertising consistently and continuously abroad, just as at home, if a product is to maintain a market. Many a direct-to-dealer campaign has aroused considerable interest and brought instant business, because with the letter was inclosed the proof of an advertisement that was to appear in the local press at a near future date. Usually the simple question, "May we add your name to the lists of dealers stocking our product?" is sufficient to elicit an initial order.

Coordinating Advertising With Sales.—An advertising campaign designed to arouse the interest of the consumer must be carefully coordinated with the sales effort. The problem is to get the dealers to stock the goods just before the advertising campaign is put on. While this is a relatively easy matter at home, it becomes somewhat difficult as the markets become more and more remote from the point where both the advertising and the product itself originate. Through a responsible advertising agency with effective associates in the country to be covered the matter can be effected with the least friction. The proposed advertising campaign will be laid out within the budget allowance agreed upon. The cities and towns in which the media circulate will be known to a nicety. The associate agency abroad, after checking the copy, can send it to the dealers in each of these cities and towns, advising them of the forthcoming campaign and sending a supply of the manufacturer's literature, prices, etc. Sufficient time will be allowed for the dealers to place orders and receive the goods before the consumer campaign is inaugurated.

Perhaps one or more jobbers, on the strength of the forthcoming campaign, will be induced to stock some of the goods so that dealers who fail to place orders may be advised where the goods may be had (at a price) after the demand has been created. As a rule, however, unless the dealer orders directly from the manufacturer, the advance he must pay the jobber for stocking the goods for him will hardly make it pay for him to purchase subsequently, even if the demand is good.

Gaining the Dealer's Confidence.—One wide-awake foreign advertising agency instructs their associates abroad to ask the dealers' advice on the general lay-out of the advertisement and to invite suggestions. This gives the dealer a much-to-be-desired sense of interest in the whole proposition and many dealers will respond to a proposal of this kind who would otherwise ignore the direct appeal of the manufacturer. In this way the advertising agency is gradually developing into a sales-promotion agency as well, supplying their clients with lists of dealers, jobbers, agents, and other potential sales outlets abroad. In this service the foreign advertising agency can be only as effective as his associate agency proves to be efficient.

As yet the foreign associate agency has much to learn before it can grasp the full meaning and intent of up-to-date American promotion methods. Many of them are still in process of evolution from the space-broker stage and it will take time and patience to educate them into real effective media of sales as well as advertising service. While it is true that sales agents are not necessarily good advertising agencies, the associate agencies abroad can be developed into broader and broader usefulness in direct-to-dealer sales campaigns by gaining the confidence of local dealers and working with them toward more effective sales effort. In the last analysis, however, the effectiveness of their work will depend upon the thoroughness of their instructions from the American agency and the grasp which the American agency shows of the local problems abroad.

Government Assistance to the Advertising Agency.—It is in strengthening this grasp of local sales conditions abroad that the Department of Commerce can be most helpful to the foreign advertising agency. Every week *Commerce Reports* contain not only helpful surveys of economic conditions cabled from the chief markets by trade commissioners and commercial attachés, but also well-written surveys of market conditions in one or more places of importance abroad. Under the commodity sections pertinent paragraphs on the markets for various commodities in the different foreign markets are supplemented by actual inquiries from foreign dealers for certain specified products in the "Trade Opportunity" section. Details regarding these inquiries, giving the names of the inquirers, their estimated annual turnover, capital and local standing can be obtained by the clients of the agencies and in time will supply a formidable dealer list. The *Commerce Yearbook* in two volumes each year furnishes the latest compiled statistics on the imports, exports, production, transportation and communication facilities, financial developments and general economic position of all the leading countries of the world. *Commerce and Navigation of the United States* is a complete record of exports and imports of products from and to the United States, by countries and commodities, as well as a record of shipping tonnage by ports. Over 400,000 Sales Information Reports on file in Washington, but available through twenty-three district offices throughout the United States, give the names of reputable agents, their size, their present agency arrangements, number of traveling salesmen, and local reputation. All of this information is available to advertising agents through their clients, provided the clients are willing and qualified as American-owned firms, to register on the Bureau's "Exporters' Index." The service is free.

Mail-Order Business Abroad.—A growing and important mail-order business has been developed through the posting of catalogues direct to consumers abroad. This development has been most pronounced in the more inaccessible regions of Brazil, Colombia, Venezuela, and other Latin-American countries, and in China in the Far East. General catalogues are mailed to China printed in English, but the Spanish catalogues sent to Latin America are usually of special types of goods. Ladies' dresses, handbags, shawls, hair ornaments, silk hosiery, etc., are the principal lines included in the Latin-American catalogues.

These catalogues are attractively and economically printed by means of the rotogravure process and afford wide distribution at nominal cost. So popular has this form of selling become in certain Latin-American countries recently that local dealers have staged protests and have sought to have the postal rates on such material raised on the grounds that mail-order houses in America pay no local taxes and should therefore not be allowed to compete with local dealers who do. Import duties on printed matter have been raised in some cases, but so far no serious reprisals have been attempted. In China and India, the missionaries, who patronize the mail-order houses extensively, have done much to create native interest in the same method of buying from abroad.

Making the Horse Drink.—From time immemorial we have heard the complaint that American sales methods are not adaptable to foreign markets and foreign conditions; that established habits and customs cannot be changed just because some alert Yankee manufacturer wishes it so. In other words, the horse may be led to water, but he will have to drink in his own fashion and when he desires. These foreign criticisms of American selling methods overlook one important fact. We have had a similar horse in our own stable for a number of years—not the same color, perhaps, with different markings, no doubt, even raised under totally different circumstances, but a horse, nevertheless. We have taught our horse to drink, and what is more important, by studying the habits of the animal we can sometimes make him want to drink, whether he is really thirsty or not. We have come to believe that if we can do this with one horse we can do it with another. We may be wrong, but many of our leading exporters have tried it with success. It may be the water, or it may be the horse. But many American exporters believe that it is the trainer who accomplishes this apparently impossible feat. Certainly we know this much—that all horses will drink if they are thirsty enough and can find the water. It is natural for a horse to drink. Therefore, to reiterate that *you can't make him* drink is somewhat beside the point. The point is *you can make him want to* drink and this is simply another way of saying that consumer demand can be created, provided the product is at all saleable.

CHAPTER VI

Selling Through Traveling Representatives

The sales or factory representative is the educator. The sales which result from his activities should be sales that could never have been effected without his aid. If the product is one that dealers will push or that consumers will demand, then the traveling salesman becomes an expensive luxury. But America is fast becoming the wonder place of the world. Out of our highly developed and complex civilization are wont to emerge, at ever increasingly rapid intervals, the mystical rabbits of the magician "Science," and while the world applauds it will not believe that they are real rabbits until the magician offers to teach them the trick.

The key to every educational campaign looking to the further sale of American merchandise abroad lies in the success of the magician in teaching his trick to his audience—the distributor. Many a high-pressure American factory representative has marked his trip throughout a sales territory with brilliant flashes of peak sales. But unless he leaves the formula indelibly imprinted upon the consciousness of the men who are to carry on after he has left, the resulting slump may more than offset the increased sales. And so the most important requisite of a successful factory representative is his ability to teach. Unless his pathway is strewn with high sales records that endure long after he has left, the manufacturer may be sure that he has not accomplished the primary purpose of his visit. He has merely exhibited his tricks but has not taught them.

Teaching Price Markets to Appreciate Quality.—The sales-promotion manager of a high-quality fountain pen recently wrote in *Export Trade and Finance:*

> "After all, the foreign manufacturer has a job to do first in Japan, and that is to educate the man behind the counter to stress quality before price, to get the trade that comes into his store to thinking generally in those terms instead of in price terms. It will be a slow, tedious process, but can be accomplished in time if the people behind counters are spurred to work assiduously at it. . . . The native salesman . . . after several days of hard study of the major selling arguments . . . that were presented to him, put on special sales in several department stores and stationers' shops, and the effect was almost immediate."

The analysis by this particular representative of the Japanese market is remarkable for the fact that he presents it to you through the eyes of the Japanese distributor, and even of the salesman in the distributor's organization, for he writes:

"And not only are the officials of these Japanese department stores interested in what reputable outside producers have to show, but their interest also carries through the lower ranks of managers and employees. Since I was was presenting an ultra grade of merchandise, the Japanese *attachés* in these stores were curious to know wherein lay the cause for the difference in price between our pens and the lower-priced lines. They were also anxious to learn the sales talk which they were to use over the counter."

Pack Peddler vs. Sales-Promotion Manager.— Trader Horn in his own inimitable style has given us a picture of the earliest type of foreign traveler. Going from house to house, approaching the back door rather than the front door, placating the consumer's dog in order to reach the consumer, the early traveler wended his weary way throughout the remote markets, earning a precarious livelihood. The rôle of the modern factory representative is quite different and his success often lies in the extent to which he realizes and practices that difference. His objective should be to organize distribution within definite sales territories. Armed with all the essential statistics before he starts, knowing the territory as well as previous experience or reading can equip him, he should start in immediately to investigate and analyze, not to sell. He should adopt the rôle of the specialist who has been called in at a good fat fee to tell the local practitioner what is really wrong with the patient. After competent diagnosis and adequate prescription he may leave.

A factory representative who is expected to effect a given increase in sales *during his stay* in the territory, becomes merely a traveling commission agent. His salary really represents his commission on his immediate sales. There are manufacturers' agents who operate on this basis. They, however, receive no salary, for they are merely expected to sell. The early pack peddler received no salary. He did not earn one. He was working for himself, not for the manufacturers whose wares he happened to be peddling. The sales-promotion manager earns a salary because he is a professional and is able to teach others what he knows.

"Making India Mosquito Conscious."—I once ran into a factory representative in a Bombay hotel. He discoursed learnedly on yellow fever, malaria, and other ailments. He seemed to have it in for the mosquito. At last I asked him just what he was doing in India, anyway.

"Making India mosquito conscious," he stated, cryptically.

"From what you've told me I should think it would be!" I exclaimed.

"Well then, I've made you mosquito conscious. I was just rattling off my sales talk. The distributors I call on always become mystified before I can show them my samples," he replied.

Whereupon he took a small can of insecticide out

of his pocket and unscrewed the top of the patent atomizer. "Squirt this on your ankles and you won't have to scratch so much," he remarked.

He then told me that he hadn't personally sold a can of the stuff in all India. His four months had been consumed in calling on dealers, arousing their interest, leaving a sample, and moving on. A day or two later a native salesman attached to the local agents who distributed his product called and booked the orders without much difficulty.

"If I do the selling," he explained, "they will expect me to call on them next month, and nobody could hire me to stay here another month—not in this climate!"

That was perhaps more true than he suspected when he said it. His employer was not hiring him to stay in India and sell insecticide. He could, perhaps, never have earned his salary. But he left a fine organization of enthusiastic dealers for the local agent to sell.

What's Rotten In Denmark?—The cost of sending a factory representative on a trip can be accurately decided in advance. I have found that my traveling expenses have run pretty close to twenty-five dollars per day abroad. This includes everything but salary. With the aid of two volumes such as those published by the Bureau of Foreign and Domestic Commerce—*Commercial Travelers' Guide to Latin America and Commerical Travelers' Guide to the Far East*—an itinerary in these two regions may be mapped out to a nicety. If the factory representative is a $10,000-a-year man, a six month's trip will cost the factory $9,500. The present volume of sales in a given territory may be $100,000 a year. Statistics may show that the factory is getting only 10 per cent of the business in that territory originating from the United States. This may be below the factory's share of the domestic business in that product. Moreover, the sales may be spotty—60 per cent in one market alone, 80 per cent in two markets, over 90 per cent in three out of twenty markets. Germany may be a wonderful market, but the question is "What's rotten in Denmark?" Is the factory willing to appropriate 9½ per cent of its sales volume with the chance of possibly doubling that volume? This is the cold, hard reasoning which should actuate the sending of a factory representative abroad. He should be equipped with the sales record of every local agent or dealer over as long a period as is available, so that he may immediately start with the ones that are falling by the wayside. If he can educate them he should do so; if he cannot, let him get others who will learn.

Intensive and Extensive Development.—Whether a traveling representative should travel ten thousand miles in six months or six thousand miles in ten months depends largely upon the problem facing the manufacturer. If the trip is to appoint new agents, the more hurried itinerary is sometimes possible. Armed with lists of the most acceptable agents and the lines they already represent, such as can be procured from the Bureau of Foreign and Domestic

Commerce, or with lists of dealers with some indication as to size supplied from the same source, the traveler, with the aid of the local offices of the American commercial *attaché,* trade commissioner, or consul, should be able to select representatives in a fairly short period. If, however, the traveler must attempt to bolster up existing agencies, to inspire old dealers with new energy, to reorganize sales forces, or to canvass distributors for educational purposes, by all means should he be allowed enough time to do the job thoroughly.

It is much better to create a first-class sales organization in a small territory than a poor one in a large territory. Moreover, the problem may be one of weeding out. Walter Wyman cites an example of a Connecticut manufacturer who cut his overseas distributors from eighteen hundred to slightly over six hundred and by the development in the export sales department of an entirely different type of assistance to dealers, increased sales at a decided decrease in sales expense. A sales organization abroad can be too extensive just as it can be too intensive. To strike the happy medium brings results.

Cutting Out Rule of Thumb.—Merely because distribution of a given product may have been successful at home or in one or two foreign markets through a given type of distributor, is no reason why the same method of distribution should be followed in all countries. As a matter of fact, it is rare that any product can be sold in precisely the same way in every market. Climate, topography, and habit alter

Langs Rhinens Vinbjerge

Som ingen anden Flod i Verden er Rhinen berømt for sin maleriske Skønhed og egenartede Stemning. Aarligt lokker den Turister til sig fra alle Jordens Lande.

De vil, hvor De end kommer frem i disse vidunderlige Egne, ingen Sinde være i Forlegenhed for korrekt Smøring med Gargoyle Mobiloil til Deres Vogn. Her – som overalt i Verden – finder De Gargoyle Forhandlere, hos hvem De kan købe det Mærke Gargoyle Mobiloil, der er det rette for Deres Motor.

Vacuum Oil Company fremstiller udelukkende Kvalitetsolier – et bestemt Mærke for hver enkelt Maskine og hver enkelt Motor – og disse Specialolier kan overalt paa Kloden købes i absolut ensartet Kvalitet. Det sikrer ethvert Automobil korrekt Smøring, hvor det end kører. Naar De bruger Deres Vogn – paa korte eller paa lange Ture – husk da, at korrekt Smøring skaaner Vognen og gør Kørselen fornøjelig.

VACUUM OIL COMPANY · A/S

Climate, Topography and Habit Alter Selling Methods and Modes of Distribution

selling methods and modes of distribution. The manufacturer who wishes to sell only to jobbers would have a difficult time finding any to sell to in some markets. Chile is the haven of the import commission house. India is often best covered, especially for "bazaar products" such as pharmaceuticals, hardware, etc., by the manufacturer's agent.

The factory representative who is hampered by rule of thumb in the home office is defeated before he starts. Let him be judged by results, not hampered by rules. The factory, it is true, may have an export policy, but export policies are sometimes good things to ignore. If distribution can be effected through types of sales representatives entirely different from those who have proven successful in other countries, learn to rely upon the factory representative's judgment. After all, that is what he is being paid for. He cannot be expected always to produce rabbits from hats. He should sometimes be permitted to produce goldfish from tablecloths. Or more important still, he cannot teach people to produce rabbits from hats where there are no rabbits and people wear no hats.

Basic Information a Safeguard.—Many a factory representative has been sent on a wild-goose chase, attempting to drum up business in territory where such business cannot possibly exist. In other cases travelers are sent out to push a product where the total volume of sales cannot possibly justify their expenses. Those things which govern sales—price, character, and extent of foreign competition, and total potential demand—should be carefully investigated before the expense of sending factory representatives abroad is incurred. These things can usually be determined by a bit of research at home or by writing to the representatives of the Department of Commerce in the fifty-five foreign trade centers where they are stationed. *Commerce and Navigation of the United States,* published by the Department of Commerce each year, gives the markets abroad for all of the more important export commodities of the United States.

If your commodity happens to be included in a classification which groups a number of minor items into a total of less than a million dollars for the lot, it is sometimes possible to obtain further details by writing to the Division of Statistics of the Department of Commerce at Washington, D. C. This figure will show what your American competitors are doing in each market. To ascertain what your foreign competitors are doing it is necessary to write to the Regional Division of the Department of Commerce, asking them to look up the total imports of your item in the returns of each of the countries showing the largest American market. Then by submitting your prices and descriptive literature to the nearest district or cooperative office of the Bureau of Foreign and Domestic Commerce you can have them forwarded to the field for comparison and report. It is only after a favorable report has been received that the sending of a factory representative to the most promising markets should be seriously considered.

Soft Drinks for Acolytes.—The manufacturers of a famous soft drink conceived the idea that their product could be marketed in those countries where the prevailing religion advocated abstinence from strong drink. They chose these countries and launched their campaign. I ran across one of their stands at the foot of the Shwe Dagon pagoda in Rangoon and found that it was patronized very freely by the yellow-robed youths who were serving their three years in the priesthood, much as young men in Europe would serve three years in the army. Although the export statistics had never shown Burma as a market for syrups, this company worked on an entirely different hypothesis. Basic statistical information, while valuable therefor, is not the only yard stick for measuring potential demand. Sometimes a considerable amount of general information, based usually on general travel and observation, is unusually helpful. Not long ago I received a call from an exporter who was complaining that his business was falling off. In the course of the conversation he happened to mention that although he had been in the export business for thirty years he had never been farther afield than the West Indies. My wonder was not that his business was falling off, but how he had been able to survive so long.

The Star-Spangled Banner.—Every American thrills at the sight of the Statue of Liberty on his return from a protracted visit abroad. That is exactly the proper time for the commercial traveler to thrill. Waving the flag, proclaiming that your factory is the "largest horseshoe-nail factory in Connecticut," are merely ways of making yourself obnoxious to those whose respect for the United States is not deepened through mere considerations of size. One traveler I knew loved to placard his dealers' offices with lithographs of the factory. These lithographs, usually produced from drawings, show rows of one-story buildings fading in neat perspective far into the background. Under this particular drawing was the boast "We cover three acres." Under it some one, presumably a competitor, had scribbled, "But we make damn bad shoes." As a matter of fact the safest thing to boast about is quality, provided it can be backed up by facts. Size of factory, quantity produced, and length of time established very seldom have the effect on the foreign mind that do proofs of quality. With price competition from Europe reviving in many lines, America's reputation abroad is being based more and more on quality and nothing can be lost by stressing it.

CHAPTER VII

PREPARING THE SALESMAN'S WAY

THE announcement of a sales representative's visit to a given foreign market is usually desirable. In rare instances surprise visits are paid by sales representatives, but little is to be gained from such visits unless the manufacturer has reason to believe that the policies or practices of the dealers are not those of the manufacturer or that malpractice is afoot. Even under such conditions secrecy is not entirely essential, for if the policies of the company have not been followed by its dealers, any attempts to cover up the discrepancies before the arrival of the sales representative would be more than vain. Such murder will out and no amount of warning of the impending visit of the sales representative would be of much benefit.

In most instances the visit of the sales representative is looked forward to with some trepidation for entirely different reasons. Only too often such a visit is warning that unless more energy is displayed and better results obtained the line may be placed with other dealers. If the product is a good seller but in the hands of the wrong type of dealers, such a change will often prove beneficial. In such cases quick efforts to remedy fundamental faults will be to no avail. In the case of the dealer who is getting good results and wishes to learn how to get better ones, the visit of the sales representative is indeed a good omen. He welcomes it and realizes that better sales and greater profit are bound to result.

Advertising for Dealers.—In most markets abroad where business is not highly organized, the choice of different types of dealers is not great. The lack of a trade press often precludes the use of this media for announcing to the proper types of dealers the forthcoming visit of a factory representative. Even if such media existed in some markets the desirability of using it would be highly questionable. Manufacturers who are used to catering to the domestic market sometimes fail to realize that some dealers abroad may at the same time be importers, jobbers, and wholesalers, carrying on the different functions at one and the same time. Other dealers may also be jobbers as well as retailers, or even wholesalers and retailers at one and the same time.

The Department of Commerce in preparing trade lists of foreign dealers has attempted to indicate these distinctions, realizing how necessary it is for a traveler to know the type of distributor he is calling on. If he wishes to place his line only with importers, he does not wish to call on people who are merely retailers. On the other hand, if he is attempting dealer distribution, he would not care to offer such terms to importers as he would offer to the retailers. None of these fine distinctions can be made in advertising for dealers. The information can only be obtained from correct trade lists or by personal investigation. Probably the best arrangement, if the factory representative intends to visit the territory, is to take the best lists available with him as a guide, making his decision as to the best means of obtaining results on the spot.

Breaking the Ground.—Where advertising may be highly advantageous, however, is in breaking the news to the trade that the product is about to be introduced into the territory. This is especially true in such highly organized markets as the British, Canadian, or German markets, where classification of distributors more or less parallels our own. Such advertisements, however, should be carefully worded to attain the desired result. After the decision has been made as to the type of distribution thought desirable, such a campaign can be most effectively laid out. If the widest kind of dealer distribution is sought, daily papers may sometimes be used to advantage. Such advertisements need not announce the coming of a representative, but merely advertise the product and ask dealers who are interested to communicate with a certain address, which will, of course, be the address of the sales representative.

With a widespread dealer interest aroused in the representation of the product throughout the territory, the next decision may be whether or not an importer or sole agent cannot be interested in taking charge of the whole territory. This decision must necessarily be based on the sales policy of the company, which in turn is often determined by the nature of the product itself; the margin of profit which the local market prices allow; and the trade practices followed by similar lines. In most foreign markets, as distribution is now organized, best results with most lines can generally be obtained through agency arrangements of some sort. Unless the manufacturer maintains a paid representative in the territory, an extensive dealer organization is difficult to maintain from the factory, and the next best arrangement is a sole agency on an over-riding commission basis. To obtain a good agent, it is often necessary for the manufacturer to create dealer interest, just as, to obtain good dealers, it is sometimes necessary to create consumer interest. The difference in the two types of advertising, however, lies in the fact that consumer interest must be maintained, while dealer interest, once aroused and properly fed from consumer demand, needs little additional incentive.

"Is It Advertised?"—This question was once put to me as I sat in the retail shop of a bazaar merchant in Calcutta. I had been trying to introduce a new food product into the Calcutta market. It had been "tough sledding." None of the bazaar dealers seemed interested. At last I found one who agreed to stock the product. All arrangements had been completed. The amount of the first order had been agreed upon. The terms of sale were satisfactory. As he was about to sign the order he paused, pencil in air, and shot this "poser" at me. At first I thought he meant would I advertise in Calcutta, and I began to elabo-

"Is It Advertised?"

rate upon the policy of the company and to make promises which, I fear, sounded rather vague.

"What I mean is," persisted my customer, "do they advertise the product at home? Do they believe in advertising? Can they afford it?"

Luckily, I had fortified myself with proofs of this, and the order was duly signed.

Later I questioned the bazaar merchant as to why he insisted on this point before attempting to introduce the product.

"American manufacturers are of two kinds," he explained, "those who build up their own product through advertising and must therefore maintain quality, and those who depend upon some one else's advertising for sales, and have consequently no interest in maintaining quality. I cannot afford to handle lines in India that are not advertised in the United States, for sooner or later the quality falls off."

The Foreign Subscriber.—A number of export trade journals in the United States have extensive foreign circulation. Some American trade papers are read for their technical and market news by a considerable body of foreign readers. The object in almost every case is to scan the advertisements of these periodicals for new discoveries. These foreign subscribers have come to realize that these journals are the accepted media utilized by the manufacturer to acquaint the trade at home with innovations and new products, and these foreign subscribers are often eager to pick up new agencies.

Not all of these foreign readers are desirable

agents. A foreign postmark and a letter in Spanish referring to the advertisement of a manufacturer possibly designed for the domestic trade is no indication that the writer would make a desirable agent. He has shown but one attribute which recommends him. He is alert. Often, however, a number of such replies from a given territory will indicate the demand for a particular product in that territory and will thus furnish a valuable index for the manufacturer or exporter. In many instances, foreign merchants, on reading such advertisements, will write to their New York buyers, placing an order and asking for the agency. Even such alluring offers should be carefully scrutinized before valuable territory is tied up.

The House Organ.—One acceptable means of creating the sort of interest among foreign distributors which often attracts business is the house organ. This is, of course, particularly true where the line is extensive and the items varied. Stories of how sales successes have been achieved in the domestic market often intrigue a foreign distributor into whose hands such advertising material may fall. Among an existing organization abroad, the loyalty to the line is often cemented and the *esprit de corps* improved by such media. House organs, of course, are of all types and descriptions. While some create one sort of impression on the foreign dealer's mind, others will create an entirely different impression.

I shall never forget meeting the sales representative of a roofing material manufacturer in a Shanghai hotel lobby. He was sitting dejectedly with a copy of his firm's house organ in his hand. I inquired solicitously regarding his welfare, whereupon he entered into a tirade upon house organs in general and the particular issue which he held in his hand in particular. I finally elicited the information that some one had "pulled a boner." The enthusiastic editor of the house organ had used one of the saleman's letters home as a "pep" message for domestic salesmen, forgetting that the house organ went to foreign agents as well. In those letters home, never thinking that they would receive publicity, the sales representative had borne down rather heavily upon his own Herculean efforts to inculcate the cardinal principles of roofing salesmanship into the dense Oriental mind of his Shanghai agent. Two months later that bland Celestial read him his own criticism and their erstwhile pleasant relations were still taut.

Catalogues Abroad.—If a sales representative is to make a trip abroad for the purpose of establishing new dealers or agents, a catalogue of the company's products may profitably precede him. Export catalogues, however, are different pieces of literature from domestic. In the first place prices are best left out entirely. Catalogues have a habit of getting into the wrong hands abroad, and domestic prices in catalogues confuse and confound a foreign dealer, while in the hands of a consumer they create complications. The catalogue is merely a display room in print and should explain the quality and character of the product as eloquently as possible, *in the language of the* *country to which it is sent.* The translation, moreover, should not be left to amateurs.

I was once shown the advertising leaflet of a toilet article. It had been translated into German by some one who knew German from a dictionary, not from residence on the Rhine. Had it ever reached the hands of a respectable German *hausfrau* I feel sure that she would have been shocked. Fortunately, it was caught before it left the country and irreparable damage done. I have often wondered, however, whether unsophisticated Americans, zealously pursuing their business in an unfamiliar tongue abroad, do make as many unfortunate mistakes in speaking as they do through the printed word.

"Veni, Vidi, Vici."—Cæsar was one of Rome's foremost salesmen. He believed in creating the psychology of success and he did not leave the creation of this psychology of success to others. He wrote the history of his exploits as he performed them. No one could mistake the true nature of his successes, and his failures were always plausibly explained. Many foreign travelers today would do well to use the same method, but in a little different fashion. Through the written word much of the psychology of success which it is necessary to instill into a foreign sales organization may be imparted before the traveler reaches his territory. He can tell what has been done in other territories. He can cite new sales "wrinkles" that have proved successful at home. He can boost where boosting is deserved, and add a cautious word of warning together with a promise of full cooperation and a confidential expectation to improve results where conditions have not been so satisfactory. In a word, he can reverse Cæsar's method of proclaiming a victory and glossing over a defeat, by predicting a victory and scoffing at the thought of defeat. If he is skillful and clever with his pen he can go a long ways towards reversing Cæsar's famous message and conquer before he either comes or sees. Most of the heralding of the salesman's approach can well be done by the salesman himself. He must become a living entity to the sales organization abroad, a sort of messiah, come to deliver them from the sales sin into which they have fallen. With such an approach to his problem the victory is already his.

CHAPTER VIII

AGENTS VS. DEALERS

PERHAPS the best advice to the manufacturer who is undecided whether to undertake distribution abroad through agents or dealers is to consider his domestic sales force. What does he do at home? Would he give his sole agency for tooth-brushes for the state of Nebraska to a dealer in Lincoln? Of course not. He would either divide up the state into its logical sales territories and give a jobber the franchise for each territory, or if he appointed a sales representative for the state he would probably put him on a commission and forbid him to engage in retailing or wholesaling. He would know full well that nothing antagonizes a wholesaler or dealer so much as to have to order through another dealer or wholesaler who is his competitor. If he wished to distribute through wholesalers or dealers he would deal with them on either very restricted territory assignments or on the open-market principle. Agent and dealer distribution, like oil and water, will not mix.

Product Determines Method of Sale.—Due more to ignorance and misrepresentation than to anything else, the most common marketing error abroad is this attempt to amalgamate two diverse systems of merchandising. Either a product should be sold through dealers or the sole agency for a given sales territory should be assigned to a manufacturer's agent, combination resident salesman, general importer, or some other type of sole agent. The product itself will determine which method should be adopted.

Dealers Are Not Good Salesmen.—Paradoxical as it may sound, the truth is that dealers are, as a rule, not good salesmen. They act as a convenience for the consumer. They stock the goods so that he may select readily. The time to sell the consumer, if he can be sold at all, is before he walks into the dealer's shop. I defy any dealer, who considers himself or his clerks salesmen, to "switch" a customer, once he has been really *sold* on a given product. I have never had much patience with the "take no other" type of customer advertising. It creates the wrong pyschology in the mind of the buyer. It as much as says: "Here's your product. You know it. We've told you all about it. But listen here. P-s-s-t! Come closer! I want to give you some advice. When you go into that store across the street, be careful. They're a bunch of city slickers, those dealers. No, sir, wouldn't trust 'em as far as you could throw a bull by the tail. Why, if you're not careful, they'll actually try to sell you an inferior product and say it's just as good as ours. Don't you let 'em. If they haven't got our product you just walk out and keep on tryin' until you find an *honest* dealer who handles *our* product."

Dealer's Function to Display.—What a fine way to introduce your customer to your dealer! No wonder the dealer is licked before he starts to try to sell. But even if he weren't—even if the manufacturer gives him every advantage, it is not his function to *sell* the manufacturer's wares. It is his function to *display* them to best advantage. If this were not true there would be no national advertising. There would be no need of it. Manufacturers would spend their advertising allowances training dealers' clerks and the devil would take the hindmost. No dealer would dare handle more than one line of a given product.

Standard Products for Dealer Distribution.—Such being the case, it follows that only the goods which are standard products carrying their own selling appeal for which there is a steady and inherent demand are the proper goods to intrust direct to a dealer for distribution. As a matter of fact, they are the only type of goods he will stock in any quantity. Obviously they are the only type of goods that will move from his shelves almost automatically, and therefore the only type that should be sold to him direct from a foreign factory without the intervening aid and counsel of a manufacturer's agent.

Changing a Dealer Into a Salesman.—Take a product that requires real selling effort, such as a cash register. One of the best foreign sales agents that a well-known cash register manufacturer ever sent abroad remarked to me once: "No one ever *wanted* to buy a cash register. Talk about sales resistance! Why, in my business it's 100 per cent. You've got to *sell the customer*. We found that the average dealer abroad simply didn't know *how*. Unless a factory-trained representative was on the spot 365 days in the year, the sales simply weren't made. Often it wasn't any lack of desire on the part of the dealer. His *interest* was there, for the commission was large on each sale. But he lacked the *technique.* Once he had the technique we had to furnish the *drive,* and by that time he had become a *salesman* not a *dealer.*"

When a Dealer is Not a Dealer.—The fact is that any dealer who succeeds in building up a good business in a specialized product requiring salesmanship *is* a manufacturer's representative. If he continues to act merely as the owner of a display room and the manufacturer's agent by advertising and other appeal creates the market for him, then he continues his normal function of dealer. This is usually what happens when the product requires real salesmanship or expert distribution. Naturally, such a manufacturer's agent must be rewarded by more than the immediate commissions on his sales. He usually demands the sole agency for a territory for a definite period of years—*i.e.,* the supervision over the sales and distribution of a number of dealers within a given sales territory. This is the only assurance he can have that business he has created will not be appropriated by the manufacturer when it begins to develop; in other words, the assurance that the manufacturer will not establish a branch or appoint a salaried factory representative and reap the rewards of his effort.

Self Sellers for Dealers.—The test, therefore, of

whether to appoint dealers or agents as your distributors abroad is whether your product sells itself or whether some one will have to sell it for you. A great many American products fall nicely into the dealer-distributor category. Most American specialties in the office equipment field are self sellers. Their novelty or peculiar usefulness has a special appeal to the customer. He only has to see it to buy it. Other products like cheap watches can be sold through direct consumer appeal, and with the demand created the dealer is glad to stock them. And so it is with a great variety of our specialties not only in the hardware, office equipment, and jewelry field, but also in the branded merchandise field of foods, drugs and medicines, etc. In most of these lines the American manufacturer has the field to himself. Where competition exists, it is price competition, and the quality appeal places the American product in a separate category from its low-priced rivals.

Manufacturer's Agent as a Sales Crusader.—This is not true of a great host of other products of which cash registers have been chosen as a typical example. Here prejudice of one kind or another has to be overcome, sales resistance eliminated, selling appeal worked up. Ever since the oil lamp displaced the tallow wick some of us in this world have been trying to sell others new ideas. That is the principal job of the manufacturer's agent. He is the crusader. He doesn't merely bring a new gimcrack to the benighted native and after fiddling with it a few moments inveigle a pearl or a lump of gold from the

Polish the Right Way

THIS is the **right** way, the **3-in-One Oil** way, to clean and polish furniture, wood work and floor. The lustrous results are really wonderful. **First:** Wring a soft cloth from cold water and drop some **3-in-One Oil** on the cloth. **Then**, rub the wood along the grain, a small surface at a time. **Finally**, polish with a soft, clean cloth. Use **3-in-One Oil** for oiling and polishing your auto, for oiling your light mechanisms and for preventing rust on metal surfaces.

3-in-One

Prevents Rust - OILS - *Cleans & Polishes*

THREE-IN-ONE OIL SELECTED FOR ITS HIGH QUALITY HAS BEEN APPROVED BY THE BRITISH PUBLIC FOR 35 YEARS.

From all Grocers, Ironmongers, Stores, Chemists, Cycle Dealers and Sports Shops in **9d.**, **1/6** and **3/-** bottles, **9d.** Oilright Cans, and **1/6** Handy Oil Cans.

FREE. *Test it at our expense. Send a card mentioning the "Home Magazine" for a generous free sample and special literature.*

THREE-IN-ONE OIL CO.
(Dept. H.M.1), 4 & 5, Stonecutter St., London, E.C.4.

USUALLY IT DOES NOT TAKE LONG FOR A MANUFACTURER TO FIND OUT WHETHER HE MUST *Sell* HIS PRODUCT unsuspecting customer. His is the serious task of teaching him to wash in a bathtub, or drive around in an automobile, or play on a piano, or use a typewriter, or do any one of a thousand or one things which the native has to be *taught* to do. Or if the native is already wearing a silk hat and a collar, he must convince the native that the silk hat and collar that *he* is selling is far superior to the one the native is wearing, so that he will discard his present apparel and buy the new one. In other words he must use salesmanship.

Method of Sale Settles Itself.—Usually it does not take long for a manufacturer to find out whether he must sell his product or whether some one will come and buy it from his dealers. He need only send a product that requires salesmanship to a few dealers and watch the results. Of course, if he advertises, the results may be different. But usually if he doesn't, nothing happens. His product does not move. There it is on the dealer's shelves, but the dealer is so busy waiting on customers who have been *sold* other products and insist on having them that he has no time to go out of his way to display goods which require time and effort to sell. So gradually the goods are pushed farther and farther back on the shelves until they become shop-worn and dusty.

Profit Sharing as a Sales Incentive.—There is only one way to convert the dealer into a salesman. Offer him a bigger profit. If the commission is large enough and the product is at all saleable, the average dealer will change into a salesman like magic. Many manufacturers have tried this and the returns have been so remarkable that they have made the fatal mistake of making the dealer a sole agent for a given territory merely on the basis of gross sales. They apparently never stop to consider the effect on their other dealer customers. There is nothing more galling than to have to go to your hated competitor in a town and order your stock of So-and-so's tooth paste, meekly paying him a commission. That is what granting a territorial franchise to a dealer means, no matter how much he has been able to sell of the product himself. Much better have him close up shop and become your sales agent. He can then, at least, sell all his erstwhile competitors in an entirely new capacity. He is not competing with them.

The Dealer in a Dual Role.—Some dealers, however, have a dual personality. In India the bazaar merchant who sleeps in his retail shop at night may own large warehouses on the Hoogli into which ocean liners from all over the world unload boatloads of products for up-country distribution. These Indian bazaar merchants, however, are keen. If they are retailers in Calcutta they seldom attempt to sell other Calcutta retailers in their capacity of wholesalers. They confine their wholesale activities to Cawnpore, Lucknow, and points up the Ganges. Seldom do such merchants act as manufacturers' agents, however, and the effect of selling a retailer in one town at wholesale for distribution elsewhere is by no means fraught with the same consequences as appointing a retail dealer sole agent for a given sales territory.

Dealer Discount as a Sales Factor.—Most manufacturers make the mistake of giving too small a discount to the foreign dealer, whether he be selling on open-market basis or buying from an agent. It is best to offer wide discounts to the dealers if they are being dealt with direct. Nothing will move your goods ahead of those of your competitors more quickly than a larger discount than the competitor is offering. All of the latent salesmanship in the dealer's make-up will thereby be brought to bear on your goods and this, backed up by reasonable consumer appeal, is usually a winning combination. If distribution is being effected through an agent the necessity for a generous profit to the dealer is none the less desirable. Nothing will ease the thorny path of the agent in selling the dealer more than an attractive trade discount, and both the dealer himself and the agent will be benefited by the metamorphosis of the dealer into a salesman.

Determining the Trade Discount.—In fixing the trade discount, however, it is absolutely necessary to know at what prices your competitors' goods are being offered, as well as what discounts they are giving. This is usually not difficult to learn. The average dealer, if buying direct, will have no hesitancy in telling you, for he would probably welcome the chance to make more money on your line. Indeed, dealers often advise manufacturers to raise prices to the consumer so that the dealer's discount can be boosted. If an agent is handling the territory he will be glad to investigate other trade discounts and retail prices as he realizes that with active dealer support his own profits will be greatly augmented.

Dealers Without Profit.—A large American motor-car manufacturer had recent occasion to overhaul all dealer arrangements in a Far Eastern country. Bright young men from American colleges were sent out full of head office "pep" with instructions to "get more profit." The first thing to be cut was the dealers' discount. The result was rather disastrous. Some of the dealers withdrew and took on competitive makes of cars. Others closed up shop and went out of the motor-car business entirely. The sales fell off tremendously. The mistake, of course, was fundamental. The dealers had been *robbed* of incentive rather than *instilled* with it. To add to the situation, dealers of long experience in the particular market had to submit to the ignominy of being "taught how to sell" by a group of boys just out of college. The result today is pretty near chaos. Luckily the loss to American trade is not so great as would have been the case did not American cars dominate the markets of the world. The loss to the company's stockholders, however, is already reflected in stock quotations. For it is to be assumed that with nearly half the sales of this one company abroad, the same brand of stupidity has been practiced in other foreign markets as well.

Foster the Dealer's Goodwill.—Whether he be acting as a salesman or the owner of a display room, the dealer is a most essential cog in the wheel of distribution. Even if he cannot make a sale he can spoil one, and to antagonize him is to stir up a hornets' nest. Dealer goodwill is most essential in any foreign sales campaign, and once it has been built up it is the most valuable asset that a manufacturer can have abroad. He can always appoint new agents, and if he has the goodwill of his dealers few of them will follow the old agent to other pastures. He can dethrone an agent, and if he retains the goodwill of his dealers they will be glad to place their orders with his newly appointed branch manager. But let him earn the enmity of his dealers, and even while handling his line they will do everything they can to "knock" it and "knife" it with that most sensitive of creatures, the ultimate consumer.

CHAPTER IX

Consumer Appeal

Trying to sell most products without creating consumer appeal is like trying to feed children castor oil without orange juice. They may take it once, but unless the orange juice of consumer appeal is added it will be hard to get a second trial unless the product has unusual merit. Now merit in a product is seldom recognized unless the astute salesman points it out. People, as a rule, do not want to recognize merit in a product they are about to buy. What we call "sales resistance" is nothing more than this innate feeling in most of us that as buyers we have a right to be sold. Few of us want to walk into a store and pick up an article and have to ask a sleepy clerk what it is and what it is used for and if it is better than some other product on the market. We like the brisk, snappy salesman who takes a personal interest in watching us and explaining, without our asking it, just what the particular product we are handling is, or even taking the trouble to take something off the shelf and explaining what it is. Alas! how few of us are satisfied in this manner. To the average retail salesman salesmanship is a lost art.

A Universal Appeal Through Advertising.—How then is the manufacturer of a product that requires this kind of salesmanship to appeal to the consumer? At home he has been fairly successful by the use of consumer advertising. He has been no less successful abroad. He has found that instead of depending upon the training of hundreds of thousands of his foreign dealers' salesmen to tell the story to the ultimate consumer, he tells them the story direct. He can give them the picture of what his product is and what it will do, and can give it with the same effectiveness to a million people all over the world at the same time. The confusion of tongues does not embarrass him; he can conquer immense distances and tell the same story to the red-bearded Sikh as he tells to the wild-riding *gaucho* of Argentina. The only thing necessary is that his product have universal appeal. It need not have universal use.

"The Old Family Tooth-Brush."—Take tooth paste. Twenty-five years ago the use of tooth paste was unknown outside of a few places in the world. Many of us in the United States were still using tooth powder. As a boy I still remember sneezing just as I had dusted a tooth-brush full of it and scattering dentifrice all over a new blue suit. Well, for one reason or another we graduated into tooth-paste users. Then we began to travel abroad, and tooth paste went with us. Some of us ran out of tooth paste on our travels and began to ask foreign merchants in Capetown and Shanghai why they did not carry it. They began ordering a few samples. It appealed to them and to their customers. "Jolly clever, these Americans," ejaculated our British cousins, guarding the economic frontiers of the Empire in Sydney and Bombay while they pinched off just enough and made it lie flat on the brush. The orders accumulated and our manufacturers began sending out salesmen. The salesmen sold lots of it. Then one manufacturer put on a world-wide advertising campaign. His sales mounted. Tooth paste had universal appeal. The consumer only had to be informed. He wanted to be sold. He wanted some one to lead him on, to overcome his sales resistance, to make him like it.

Dealer a Cog in Distribution Abroad.—Of course, little could have been accomplished in this world campaign for American tooth paste without the dealer. He acted as the service station in the supply of the consumer by the manufacturer and reinforcing him and supplying him were the manufacturers' agents and general importers abroad with functions corresponding roughly to those of our jobbers at home. The moving force, however, was the selling appeal of the product intelligently translated into understandable terms. This was done through advertising.

Purchasing Power a Vital Factor.—No matter how appealing a thing may be to the ultimate consumer, if he is without cash or credit with which to purchase it, the creation of the appeal is waste effort. Many of the world consumers live from hand to mouth. Of the eight hundred million people in the three countries China, India, and Russia, comprising more than half the world's population, not more than 5 per cent have stable, continuing purchasing power.

BRINGS DEEP, PEACEFUL REFRESHING SLEEP

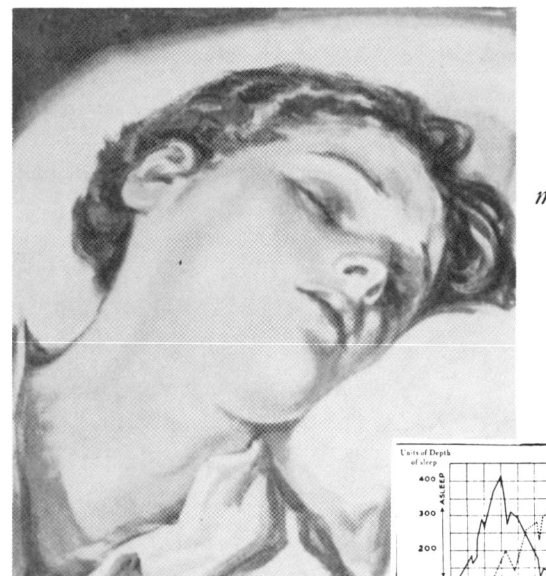

★

more restful than hours of light, broken slumber

★

Units of Depth of sleep

400 300 200 100

ASLEEP AWAKE

12 PM 1 2 3 4 5 6 7 8

Such profound rest alone banishes fatigue

TOSSING, turning, restless, wakeful . . . what hours of weary discomfort the night can bring!

"Sleeplessness," doctors say, "is a growing menace." Investigations show that 70 out of 100 people living in large towns today suffer from lack of restful sleep.

Noise, lack of fresh air and exercise, worry — all the stress and strain of modern life, tend to make us restless and wakeful at night. Even if we sleep, too often our sleep is poor in quality, restless and unrefreshing, so that when we wake we have not fully shaken off the fatigue of the previous day.

There is a simple way to ensure restful sleep — a way that doctors themselves use and recommend — by drinking a hot cup of Horlick's last thing at night.

As you sip the delicious drink, its generous warmth penetrates and soothes your whole system.

Warmed, soothed and fed, you are in the mood for slumber — drowsy and relaxed, you are soon soundly asleep.

While you sleep, Horlick's is storing your body with precious nutriment: proteins from rich milk, carbohydrates from fine wheat and malted barley — the ingredients Horlick's is made from. Yet so digestible is Horlick's — many times more easily assimilated than ordinary cows' milk — that it lays no strain on the digestive organs.

After a night of such sound, refreshing sleep, you wake feeling relaxed and rested, full of energy for the day's work.

Start taking Horlick's this very night! Almost immediately you will find that you sleep better, and will wake feeling fitter and fresher for the coming day. There are two delightful varieties — plain Horlick's Malted Milk and the new Chocolate Flavoured kind. Mix your drink with the Horlick's Mixer. It tastes doubly good made this way.

Chemists and grocers have Horlick's in sealed glass bottles in four sizes.

Contrasting curves illustrating (a) deep sleep, (b) light sleep.

In refreshing sleep the "maximum depth" is reached early in the night. In restless sleep, the sleeper takes longer to reach the point where he is most soundly asleep. "Sleep tests" prove that the lighter the sleep the greater the difficulty, once awakened, in getting to sleep again.

Horlick's at bed-time helps one to fall soundly and quickly asleep

HORLICK'S · PLAIN *or* CHOCOLATE FLAVOURED

THE ONLY THING NECESSARY IS THAT HIS PRODUCT HAVE UNIVERSAL APPEAL

The rest are so close to actual starvation all of the time that nothing can appeal to them except the very primary wants of food and clothing. Other peoples of the world present higher percentages of purchasing power, but nowhere, with the possible exception of England and parts of the British Empire, is there the purchasing power that exists in the United States. Advertising appeal should be gauged accordingly. Consumer demand can be created in many places where it cannot be satisfied.

Buying Seasons and Consumer Appeal.—In some places in the world consumers have money to spend at certain times of the year and not at others. This is particularly true of agricultural countries where harvest time corresponds roughly with the period of greatest purchasing power. It is then that farmers have money to spend, when an appeal created is most likely to result in a desire satisfied. Many manufacturers, therefore, time their appeals to consumers so that they will create a desire for their product at this time of greatest purchasing power. They wait for the money to reach their customers' pockets before they try to sell him. But when they do want to sell him, he must see and feel and test the product he has been told about through the printed word. The manufacturer must therefore arrange to have stocks of his goods where the consumer can see them at the time that he is able to buy. Then he must appeal direct to the consumer and tell him about the goods.

Stocking the Dealer for the Buying Season.—Buying seasons vary with local crop and weather conditions. In the temperate zones they come usually in the spring and the fall. In the tropics they sometimes come more often. No matter when they come the dealer must have the manufacturer's goods on his shelves at that time if he expects to get the maximum sales. Moreover, for several months before, if the product has universal appeal, the consumer should be reached, if he can read, through the various consumer media, and if he is illiterate through pictures and by the familiar medium of the ballyhoo or direct word-of-mouth appeal. Unless both the stocking of the goods and the appeal are correctly timed a great deal of effectiveness will be lost. This is the most difficult phase of overseas selling. To do it correctly with a product distributed throughout the world requires a mass of facts difficult to obtain and not easy to assimilate. Without a correct timing of consumer appeal and the stocking of dealers much ill will can be created and sometimes years of patient work must be expended to overcome a single miscalculation.

Making Mountains Out of Molehills.—Not only is the place and time important in creating consumer appeal, but the method must be correct. To the untried exporter the glib appeal of his foreign agent to allow him a percentage of sales for advertising is often reinforced by the argument that, after all, local taste differs all over the world and no one ten thousand miles away can possibly word an appeal that will exactly fit every locality. This may have been true twenty-five years ago. It may have been true before the motion picture and now the sound picture had brought Hollywood and Broadway to Surabaya and Johannesburg. But it is not true today. One world-wide advertiser has told me that they find exactly the same advertisement creates exactly the same results from Timbuctoo to Tipperary. The world has grown so close together that a pulling advertisement designed for Iowa will bring in customers in Montevideo with equal effectiveness.

Of course, many absurd mistakes have occurred in the past. There is the classic instance of the manufacturer of automobile horns who naïvely advised his potential customers in Australia of the "resounding warning reverberating from hill to hill," while the joyous motorist "wound slowly up mountain-side and down into valley." The native Australian gazing at a flat horizon probably wondered only whether the horn would scare the rabbits from his path.

Local Color Versus High Costs.—Not only is the modern foreign advertising agency in the United States fully equipped to prevent their clients from making such mistakes, but the savings effected through low mat and plate costs in the production of cuts for a hundred or more periodicals and newspapers throughout the world in one central place, are no mean item. Even with these advantages the proponents of local agents for the handling of foreign advertising insist that copy prepared locally has much greater appeal and drawings made by local artists go over with the local consumer, where the imported variety falls flat.

The Associate Agency One Solution.—The solution to this vexing problem which continues to divide the ranks of the advertising fraternity probably lies in the use of the associate agency by the American agency. In this way all of the economies of mass production in the preparation of copy, drawings, mats, and cuts can be effected; the standard character of the appeal can be maintained and the best results obtained from domestic copy employed abroad, while the associate agency abroad checks the copy for local appeal, consults with the local agent for local selling arguments lending a domestic flavor to the standard advertisement, and finally places the advertisement with the local media at rates arranged under a large space contract by the American agency.

"O-o La! La! Oui, Oui."—Andrew G. Billings in the November, 1929, issue of *Advertising Abroad* cites the following pertinent instance of the value of maintaining the home flavor in foreign advertising:

> "Paris is supposed to be the headquarters for style and make-up, and the French manufacturers of toilet preparations, ladies garments, etc., do a thriving business with the American feminine market-places of New York, Chicago, Cleveland, and points East, West, South, and North. Do these advertisers, in their copy appeal, attempt to disguise their home nationality? Emphatically, they do not. Americans may write the copy, but in doing so they make it sound like a literal translation from the French, even to the inclusion of a few choice untrans-

lated phrases. *N'est-ce pas?* Catch them overlooking the real appeal of Paris in the American market!"

Diverse Conditions Make Localized Copy Impracticable.—Regarding consumer appeal abroad Mr. Billings continues:

"But many of these people want our goods because they believe that American standards of production enable the best quality of goods to be turned out and because they regard American standards of living to be worth emulating, even to the extent of themselves demanding the sort of goods these standards call for and obtain. American motion pictures have been great missionaries in this respect, although not with any commercialized intention.

"Those who prepare the copy for American advertising abroad must, if they are to do a real job, be possessed of adequate knowledge of local needs and customs with respect to the product they wish to sell, not merely in all the countries in which the advertising is to appear, but in the various districts of any one country; for both needs and native psychology vary much more widely abroad than they do at home within given territorial limits. There are no *Saturday Evening Posts* in Borneo or the Fiji Islands.

"This information must come from many courses to the hand of the man who *directs* the copy appeal. No one man can obtain it from first-hand experience, for he can have been born only in one locality and really be familiar, at the best, with the actual districts in which he has lived and worked.

"Perhaps the real answer to 'Who should write the copy?' is to be found in the American specialized foreign agency, with its facilities for obtaining accurate information from many sources regarding local needs and psychology; with its merchandisers who can properly shape the campaign as a whole and direct the copy-appeal angle; and its specialized translators who are able to put this into the proper vernacular.

"But hesitate a bit before eradicating all of the Americanism from your copy appeal, for there, perhaps, may lie its strongest single element."

The Plea for Local Copy Writing.—The advocates of the local copy-writer are not to be quieted, however, with any such argument. In the same issue of *Advertising Abroad* José Fajardo presents the side of the local colorists with a strong appeal:

> "Advertising copy [he says], to be effective, must approach its prospect like a casual acquaintance who meets you unexpectedly, speaks in the familiar drawl of your section, and promises good news of the home town and your old friends. It must gain your sympathy in the short moment that you read it. Any hitch or strange accent can spoil that momentary feeling

> of sympathy and snatch away any chance for your message. How then can any export copy carry a genuine sales appeal unless it sounds psychologically familiar to the readers? How can it belong with the readers unless it be prepared by a person who is one of them—who understands their ways of thinking?"

He then goes on to cite instance after instance of actual copy "Made in America" which carries strange symbols of a civilization not in tune with local conditions abroad. Not only does Mr. Fajardo recommend native copy-writers, but also local sales representatives for American manufacturers abroad rather than the type of Americans so often sent abroad to represent American houses.

"Know Your Audience."—His conclusions are interesting:

> "It is therefore an impossibility for the average American, educated or otherwise, not to retain an attitude that balks him from thinking that foreign ways of thinking and living can be good or even worthy of consideration. Little wonder when we have installed in our minds the belief that we are a godly people in a God-blessed country, destined to impose our civilization, religion, morals, and customs on the rest of humankind. Far from antagonizing this attitude, I mention it here only because it is what kills any flicker of real salesmanship that a prospective Spanish copy-writer, American-born,

can have. It is an impregnable wall to the first requirement of the advertising profession—Know Your Audience. . . .

"As far as I know, advertising experts, directors, and books treating the subject of export, when probing the matter of export copy, invariably conclude that copy prepared by American writers, and translated with minor changes in the necessary language, is as good as, and often superior to, copy prepared any other way. The isolated instances they mention, in my opinion, fail to prove their contention. Some good French or Spanish copy, translated into English, might possibly make a hit with American people, but would this justify using translated copy in America, as a rule? This equally applies to Latin America or any other foreign country; copy to *reach* the readers must be written by one close to their ways of thinking, their mode of living, their racial heart."

Keeping the American Appeal.—Another interesting phase of this controversy is discussed by J. Francis Dement of the Dictaphone Corporation in the same periodical.

"If the native is looking for tooth paste, cosmetics, or office appliances and wants American goods, it is for some specific reason. He therefore looks for advertisements describing such products, and he is attracted by those where the background, as well as the article, is American.

"The foreigner purchases automobiles, flash-lights, and other products manufactured in the States because they have certain outstanding features in design and utility which are of first importance. It follows that his attention would be drawn to this article much more readily if the individuality of advertising followed the individuality of the article. And this can be done only by portraying subjects of a type customarily in use in the United States.

"Respect is not founded on aping the customs of other people. American merchandise abroad has won the respect of the foreign markets because of its manifest advantages. If that were not true, our manufacturers would be copying the styles and designs of our competitors. Therefore why not carry this individuality, which has proven successful in disposing of our products, to our advertising, thus completing the cycle?"

Let Your Conscience Be Your Guide.—And so the controversy rages. The manufacturer who is faced with the problem of deciding upon the type of copy-writer he will employ will no doubt be guided by considerations quite foreign to those that have been advanced. The whole matter of handling advertising copy abroad has become a specialized profession. It is no longer possible for the tyro to strike gold with a pick-ax. Competition is too keen. Unless, therefore, the prospective advertiser has a highly developed advertising department of his own, he would be well advised to leave decisions as to the details of copy-writing to a well-organized foreign advertising agency. Even with a domestic advertising department, foreign advertising is a distinct departure in the advertising field and has a developed technique of its own. Even the advocates of American copy-writers, it is noted, admit the necessity of wide knowledge of foreign conditions on the part of the person who directs the work. If the manufacturer were about to change the layout of his factory he would probably consult the best efficiency engineer he could find. If he had an important lawsuit pending he would not leave the case in the hands of a clerk in his legal department. He would engage the best counsel available. Nothing could be more important in embarking upon a sales campaign abroad than the type and character of his advertising appeal. He wants to put his best foot forward abroad. He has a reputation to build. He must give the presentation of his case to the foreign consumer the best that is in him. No advice is too good under those circumstances. No expenditure too great.

CHAPTER X

When to Establish a Branch Abroad

"All's not gold that glitters."

Many an agent or distributor has built up his principal's business abroad until it looked like a gold mine. The 10 or 15 per cent commission which the agent was drawing out of the business has amounted to a tidy sum each year. Under such circumstances it may pay the manufacturer to consider seriously the opening of a branch. It is all not so simple as that, however. His business has been built up through the efforts of human beings, and human beings are resentful creatures when they believe they have been wronged. If he is ruthless and cuts off his agent, he must expect the natural resentment and reprisal that such action may justify. Remember the manufacturer has only supplied the goods. The actual contacts have been made by the agent. He knows the dealer clientele. They are his friends and his fellow-countrymen. Many of them will follow him if he is "let down." Many of them may turn against American products altogether. When the manufacturer is doing well with an agent abroad, he has no positive assurance that he can do well with a branch. The figures may prove that he can, but figures are notorious liars. He must consider the welfare of his agent in the new scheme of things. He must not forget the human element.

Time to Re-Tire.—A certain tire company—NOT the one using the above slogan, however—had built up a splendid business abroad along agency lines. When the agents began to collect commissions each year which were more than enough to finance the opening of branches, the company one day calmly announced a change of policy, threw all its agents overboard, and opened its own branches. The effect was disastrous not only to its own business, but to that of the other American tire companies selling abroad. The ex-agents promptly obtained the agency for a British tire and took most of their former dealers with them. The result was that a ten-million-dollar business dwindled in one year to less than a tenth of its former proportions and the other American tire companies have found it difficult ever since to obtain and hold good agents.

Be Reasonable With the Agent.—The facts are that foreign agents, being human beings, are open to reason. If they see that their commissions are mounting to a point where it would be more profitable to put them on a salary, in other words make them branch managers, most of them are amenable to reason. Some would accept part of their previous territory and continue to function as distributors under the branch. As a matter of fact the average agent abroad has only a few lines which are known as "bread and butter" lines. In other words, the agencies from which he makes the lion's share of his income will often number only two or three. If your line happens to be his best and he sees a chance of losing it unless he forsakes the others and enters your employ or takes a restricted territory, the chances are that he will give the matter grave consideration. Too many manufacturers are prone to assume that the agent would not even listen to their proposition. It is best to give him a chance. If after you have offered him the branch managership or restricted territory and he refuses it, you appoint some one else, then you, at least, have not alienated the sympathies of your dealers and you can place your case before them and appeal for their support.

Sending a Boy to the Mill.—Another consideration is the question of personnel for the new branches, if the agents are not to be considered. Many manufacturers argue that if they open a branch abroad they want some one who has been trained in their own factory and who knows their production difficulties. The agent, they say, is often unreasonable in his demands for delivery because he does not know the problems of production. He will promise a dealer anything to get the order and then expect the factory to perform. To overcome this difficulty they want their own man as foreign branch manager and many of them base their action in upsetting agency relationships on none other than these considerations. From the point of view of the production manager these arguments may be valid enough. But from the sales angle they should carry little or no weight.

The agent is more than likely a man of broad sales experience. If he has built up the business to the point where it warrants the opening of a branch, he must know the territory thoroughly and be on the best of terms with his dealers. If such a man were branch manager the manufacturer would think twice before replacing him with a young man from the factory who was entirely green to the territory and had no connections whatever. Yet American manufacturers have done just this thing time and time again abroad and then have wondered why their sales have fallen off. A sales organization is a fearful and wonderful thing, and to tamper with it is like tampering with the human body. The results are likely to be distressing.

"Show Me the Way to Go Home."—A west-coast exporter had built up a fine business in Singapore through an agent. His arrangement was that the agent traded under the exporter's name, but was actually operating on a commission basis. The principal of the export house died and his son undertook to "reorganize the business." He canceled the agreement with the Singapore agent, assuming that as the business was under the American firm name anyhow, it would make no difference. He sent a very young and very unsophisticated clerk from his office to Singapore as branch manager. The old agent had built up an enviable reputation for fair dealing among the Chinese dealers and he was well beloved by the community. Naturally, the reception given the youngster was chilly. He found it hard to join the clubs and he was not invited to social gatherings. Through no fault of his own, for he was personally a very fine, clean-living chap, he was more or less ostracized. The business fell off from month to month. The old agent, backed by friends, started in on his own and carried most of his dealers with him. He had no difficulty in making arrangements for competing agencies from the United States. The luckless youth who had been sent out as branch manager stuck it out for a year and then took a steamer for home. Today the American firm which for a decade had held a leading place in Singapore's trade no longer exists.

Retain the Agent's Enthusiasm.—If an agent is approached to become a branch manager it must be remembered that he built up the business to its present proportions with the incentive of a commission on sales. It is not wise to remove that incentive entirely. The best arrangement and one that has worked successfully in a number of cases is to arrive at the salary of the agent on the basis of his present business. Ascertain what his expenses have been, what the interest on his investment is, and what has been his net income. If possible make him an offer that approaches his net income. Then with his last annual sales volume as a basis, offer him an overriding commission on all sales in excess of his best effort. In other words, retain his incentive to produce. Nine times out of ten you will not regret it.

Many agents abroad aspire to become branch managers for one of their best lines. It enables them to devote their entire time to a single commodity and to perfect themselves in the sales technique of a single group of related items. It does not divide their effort. In most instances they can accomplish more by concentrating their energies than they can by spreading them over a number of lines. By all means give the conscientious agent a chance to make good. He deserves it and should be encouraged to look forward to the time when his sales volume will reach such proportions as to warrant his reward in the form of a branch managership. No manufacturer who overlooked his agent's rights and interests has found that it paid.

Branch Management vs. Agency Control.—An important consideration governing the decision to establish foreign branches to replace agencies is the set-up of the export department itself. The type of successful export manager who can control and guide a group of agencies abroad is not necessarily the same type as would most successfully manage a group of foreign branches. Agents are independent entities; their expenses are matters of their own concern and not that of the manufacturer; they can be told to do this and that to get sales and they must use their own judgment in the last analysis as to whether the added expense will be justified in greater sales volume.

With a branch manager this is not necessarily so. He is operating under direct instructions from headquarters. The sales expense he incurs is usually based upon the judgment of the responsible official in charge of export sales. If mistakes of judgment are made they are frequently made over his protest and in accordance with some rigid sales policy which an adamant and rule-of-thumb executive dictates often in total ignorance of local conditions abroad. For these reasons many a successful foreign sales executive under a system of foreign agency distribution has proven to be a "total flop" when he attempted to manage a chain of foreign branches. The establishment of foreign branches should come, therefore, as a rule, only after years of export experience on the part of the entire organization, when foreign sales executives have been thoroughly seasoned by frequent trips abroad and have a fairly broad acquaintance with conditions in each of the principal sales territories.

The Quota System of Branch Sales.—Various devices for retaining the sales incentive in addition to the over-riding commission have been successfully applied by some of our leading export manufacturers. The quota system, so useful at home, can be applied with equal effectiveness in the foreign field. Where a branch is established in place of an agency, the quota is fairly easy to establish. It is not always good policy to accept the turnover of an agent as the standard performance for a given territory, even though his record may have proven highly satisfactory. Some agents work under handicaps that branch organization may avoid. Their dealer clientele may have been limited by the size of their sales organization and the extent of its operations. Investigation may prove that a comparatively small addition to the traveling sales force, the rerouting of salesmen and the readjustment of sub-agency territory will greatly enlarge the dealer clientele and warrant the setting up of a much larger sales quota for the whole area.

The quota system, unless scientifically adjusted, can cause as much havoc in branch sales management as it frequently causes when faultily applied to agency distribution abroad. It can act as a deterrent rather than an incentive to sales activity if placed too high, or as an excuse for "soldiering" if placed too low. Unless quotas are based on something more than educated guesses on the part of sales executives many thousands of miles from the scene of actual operations, they had much rather be dispensed with altogether.

The "Open End" Agreement.—A fairly accurately adjusted sales quota accompanied by an arrangement for commission over salary on all sales over the quota is often an ideal arrangement for branch-management operation. A large manufacturer of office equipment made such an agreement with a newly appointed factory-trained representative whom they sent to Japan. He was paid a basic salary which was enough to live on, and his quota was fixed at the last year's sales of the agent. He did not supersede the agent, which was a large trading company, but under an arrangement with the company and the agent, worked for them. Their commission was a straight 5 per cent for financing, delivery, and collection. The factory representative's commission ranged from 5 per cent on the first increase of 50 per cent to 20 per cent when the increase had reached 200 per cent. At the end of the third year, when his agreement terminated, the factory representative had increased the annual turnover about 250 per cent and his salary and commission so far exceeded the commission paid the agent or any of the local managers of the agent's organization that he was brought back "as a disorganizing influence." The manufacturer had a long-term agreement with the agent and thought that with the sales organization established by the factory representative the profits would be much greater if the factory representative were out of the picture altogether when his agreement expired. The effect of his removal was instantaneous. His personality and magnetism had held the sales force to a high level of performance. Under the stultifying influence of the agent's organization the sales soon returned to what they had been before the factory representative appeared.

The Personal Equation.—Enough has been said to indicate the enormous variability of the personal equation in direct sales management abroad. Unless, therefore, the manufacturer is sure of his men and their foreign training, he would be better advised to leave well enough alone even though his agents appear to be making inordinate profits from his line. Selling costs in many foreign markets are often much higher than in the United States; transportation is more expensive for travelers; advertising expense is often greater and the payment of customs duties, gratuities to officials, and other expenses now borne by his agent are often overlooked in figuring the net profit. Too often the manufacturer will deduct from the commissions he has paid an agent a percentage representing sales cost in the United States and decide to open his own branches on the difference. Too often he finds, when it is too late, that sales cost in many foreign markets is twice and three times what it is in the United States and his branches become a burden under inexpert management and finally a loss.

"All's not gold that glitters."

CHAPTER XI

Foreign Branch Advertising

The advertising policy of a manufacturer distributing abroad through branches differs little in principle from that of the manufacturer using agents. Certain considerations, however, enter into the problems of foreign advertising when branches are used for foreign selling which are not present under agency arrangements. The branch is the local office of the manufacturer. The nature of its personnel, the character of its service, and the very appearance of the physical layout reflects the home factory to the foreign dealer. So with the advertising.

The fact that a branch exists in a given foreign city in a sense transplants the factory to the local setting. The factory is no longer merely represented abroad. Its own branch manager has become part of the local community. He has certain civic responsibilities. He is amenable to local jurisdiction and hence his home office is subject to greater surveillance through his acts than it was through the acts of its agent. The local manager cannot escape criticism if an advertising campaign improperly managed from home places him in a ludicrous position. He is expected to have some authority and influence with the home office in the matter of advising what is and is not proper. Mistakes that might not jeopardize the position of the agent will invariably be laid at the door of the branch manager. He will be held to account both by the dealers and by the consumer for any breach of international etiquette, and may even feel the effects of political acts over which neither he nor his company has any control.

Motor-Cars for Ladies.—A large motor-car manufacturer put out a new model, the selling feature of which was the fact that it could be easily controlled by the supposedly weaker sex. It played up these features in its domestic advertising with distinct success. An ingenuous advertising agency was intrusted with the task of putting over the new model abroad. Without consulting any of the many branches of the manufacturer abroad or any foreign associate agency, it placed long contracts with foreign media direct, using practically the same cuts and copy that had been so successful at home. Imagine the chagrin of the branch manager in Buenos Aires when his choice prospects were told in no uncertain terms that the *duenna* could manage the car with perfect safety, that changing a tire was the matter of a moment! The grand dames of the Argentine snorted in rage and their husbands canceled contracts for cars ordered months in advance. They would not have their wives treated to such indignities. What sort of a Yankee insult was this, anyway!

The branch manager not only lost most of his sales for months ahead, but dared not go near his club. The response to his frantic cables to the factory was that the advertising agency had the matter in hand and they didn't understand what all the fuss was about, anyway. Finally the branch manager resigned and went home, but the long-contract advertisement still ran gayly on in the best newspapers and magazines of the South American capital.

Making the Eagle Scream.—It is a well-known fact that some of the most rabid anti-American dailies in British India have for years subsisted principally on the largess from the advertising appropriations of American manufacturers. Branch managers of large distributors in India have pointed out the harm that these anti-Yankee tirades have done to the business of the manufacturer and have suggested a closer relationship between the placing of advertising and the management of sales. The danger that lurks in such a course, however, is keenly appreciated by most manufacturers. The withdrawal of copy on any other than pure business grounds would be likely to cause a reaction and a criticism that would do more harm than good.

Where joint action can be taken, as in the case of an exceptionally rabid Yankee-baiting daily in the Punjab, however, the results have been instantaneous. If the branch manager were given some say in the selection of local media, he could often remedy many such conditions in a diplomatic way without taking any overt action. One thing is certain, American advertising means the spending of many millions of dollars abroad each year and this money goes directly into the coffers of the most influential of local media throughout the world. As every advertising man knows and as no newspaper will admit, publicity of a favorable and helpful nature can often be arranged and is better than paid advertising under many circumstances. Such matters can hardly be arranged through an agency, even though its associates abroad are the best. They can be arranged through the local branches abroad, and the manufacturer who does not use his branches in this manner is often losing much of the best effects that his paid advertising can obtain.

The Shoemaker and His Last.—The establishment of branches abroad in no way dispenses with the services of the foreign advertising agency. The same considerations which make it undesirable for the agent to handle local advertising apply with equal force to the branch. The branch manager cannot effect the economies of the American advertising agency in the matter of art work, cuts, or even copywriting. What is more important, the branch manager is not an advertising man and should not be expected to perform the functions of one. He is a valuable adjunct to any advertising campaign, however, not only in the initial stages of planning its scope, but in checking over the copy and even passing on the art work and seeing that it conforms to local prejudices and tastes. The foreign advertising agency that does not use the branch manager either through direct contact or through its foreign associates or branches abroad is not doing its job properly. Many foreign advertising agencies realize this

Its tread extends down the sidewalls, that's one reason why the Goodyear Motor-cycle Tyre is preferred by the keen motor-cyclist. When he swings his machine over to corner at speed, that tread grips. It doesn't slip. It saves valuable seconds that may make all the difference between " fastest time of the day " and " also ran."

Tough—buoyant—enduring—there's everything in this tyre to make it ideal for every motor-cyclist.

MADE IN ENGLAND

The Goodyear Tyre & Rubber Co. (Great Britain), Ltd., Wolverhampton
Factories in: England, Australia, Canada and United States

THE ESTABLISHMENT OF BRANCHES ABROAD IN NO WAY DISPENSES WITH SERVICES OF THE FOREIGN ADVERTISING AGENCY and not only maintain close contact with the foreign branches of their clients, but even send their representatives abroad periodically to confer with the foreign branch managers and agents of their clients. Certainly no world-wide campaign of any magnitude should be planned without first consulting every foreign branch manager and getting the local angle on every phase of the work, including media, appeal, time, extent, copy, and art work.

The Nemesis of the Punkah-Puller.—I once met the representative of a large American electrical manufacturer in Bombay. He was spending several months in India and occupied his time at the office of the local distributor with a desk piled high with voluminous government reports on temperature, of which nature has bestowed a varied selection for the benefit (or blight) of the benighted Hindu.

"What on earth are you studying?" I asked one day, unable to restrain my curiosity longer.

He leaned back, pushed aside a huge blue paper-bound volume, and lit his pipe.

"The weather," he replied. "Believe it or not, we don't know a thing about it."

"I do," I gasped, wiping a perspiring brow. "I know all about it."

"Then tell me," he challenged, "how hot it gets in Amritsar in April."

"Too hot," I remarked.

He laughed and pulled out a long graph. A dozen wavy lines crossed it in dazzling irregularity.

"What are those," I asked, "heat waves?"

"No," he replied. "Temperature variations of the twelve largest cities of India. You see, we want to put on our advertising campaigns for electric fans at the times that they will do the most good."

No advertising agency in America probably had at that time the information shown on those graphs, yet it seemed essential to the proper conduct of an advertising campaign for electric fans in India.

Dealer Advertising and the Branch.—In advertising to the dealer, the cooperation and assistance of the branch manager is most desirable. It is his immediate duty to attract and hold the dealer. Not only is the timing of the dealer advertising campaign almost entirely a matter of branch sales control, but the very wording of the appeal, its approach, and the arguments used are matters which must conform in every respect to the ideas and plans of the branch manager. Naturally the local aspect of the whole campaign is one that will appeal to most dealers. If they feel that a branch in one of the large cities of their territory is immediately concerned with sales, is possibly stocking goods or replacements, and is so situated as to give them service quickly and efficiently, they will be much more interested in placing orders than if the appeal is staged from a distance of ten thousand miles and they are merely given the name of a local agent.

One of the large oil companies made a tremendous hit in India by advertising *service* rather than quality or price. They emphasized the quick deliveries to the most remote points in almost any amounts. The response was immediate, for dozens of industries throughout India used large amounts of lubricating oil, but due to the use of native foremen it was difficult for the management to keep an accurate check on supplies which were constantly running short. By stressing service, quick delivery, and large stocks on hand, the oil company through its advertising campaign built up a demand that its branches were bound to fill. Such a campaign, however, could only be carried on with the closest cooperation of the branch managers and dealers in order to prevent disappointments in delivery.

The Consumer and the Branch.—Consumer advertising abroad, while not requiring the same close cooperation with the branch, must nevertheless conform in all respects to the branch manager's selling policy and plans. Foreign branches, unless consulted on every aspect of the foreign advertising within their territories, often find themselves embarrassed. A typewriter manufacturer decided to put out a new model. A world-wide advertising campaign was planned, and in time the branches throughout the world read the advertisements in their local papers. They were interested, but there were no deliveries. Shipment after shipment arrived, but not a new model. Finally, dealers began asking for the new model and customers began refusing to buy old models. Sales fell off because people wanted the new model and were willing to wait for it. But the new models didn't arrive. At last branch managers began cabling to rush the new model. The answer came back that due to a hitch in the production schedule they could not possibly be shipped within three months. Somewhere along the line between the production department and the advertising department there had been a bad slip-up. With a little cooperation the error might have been avoided. Had the branches had some say in the matter of releasing the campaign locally, they could have timed the advertising to appear shortly after the arrival of the first shipments. As it was, much of the effect of the campaign was lost and many disappointed customers bought other makes.

Building Branch Sales Through Advertising.—Every branch manager abroad should be the most enthusiastic believer in advertising and should seek voluntarily to aid the advertising department and foreign advertising agency by helpful suggestions. The foreign advertising agency which, through false pride in its own equipment, fails to enlist the most active cooperation from its client's foreign branches and agents, is not up to its job. It is often the rôle of the management to see that this close liaison is effected and that it works properly, that the personal equation is properly balanced, and that a clearing-house for information and suggestions is established, if necessary, in either the advertising or the export department. Direct contact between foreign advertising agency and foreign branch can often be effectively set up, particularly if the foreign advertising agency works through foreign associates or branches. Unless the relationship works smoothly, the most effective work cannot be expected in advertising and selling abroad.

CHAPTER XII

Conclusion and Summary

The formulation of a foreign sales campaign should follow a definite plan. First the extent of the possible market abroad should be definitely judged. The selection of foreign agents should be deliberate and not haphazard. The same principles in agency selection which have proven successful at home can be used to advantage abroad. The selection of the type of agent or distribution method is as important as the selection of the distributor himself. Unless all these things are taken into account before any attempt is made to enter the foreign market, much grief is almost certain to be experienced, much waste effort expended.

Getting the Foreign Picture.—The first step in any export campaign should be a thorough consideration of *all* markets—their population, methods of distribution; their exports, imports and the countries of destination and origin; the balance of their trade, including merchandise and invisible items; the trend of trade, whether increasing or decreasing. The foreign picture, its potentialities and possibilities, can only be adjudged properly if all the important facts are well in mind. All of this information is easily accessible. It is essential that it be reviewed with an eye to its relationship to the marketing of the particular line under consideration before even the first steps to obtain agents are undertaken.

Determine the Type of Distributor.—There are innumerable combinations of methods of foreign distribution. Most of them, however, can be classified into about three major groups: the salesman-dealer method, the traveler-agent method, and the branch office. There are all sorts of salesmen to be utilized and they may call upon many types of dealers. There are a multitude of foreign travelers who may appoint many varieties of agents. Branches may be semi-agencies or full-fledged branches. The particular method of distribution must depend primarily upon the type of product and secondarily upon the extent to which the exporter wishes to develop his foreign business immediately.

When to Use Dealers.—Staples changing in style and subject to little price fluctuation can often be sold through dealers because jobbers and wholesalers are willing to stock them, and dealers, as a rule, desire to order from local stocks. Routing a salesman to call on foreign dealers is a matter of exact planning, both that he may arrive at the peak of the selling season and that he may cover as much territory as possible economically. If dealers are to be used for direct distribution, therefore, arrangements must be made for salesmen to call on them periodically and at the right time. Only products of a very specialized nature can be sold to dealers by mail.

When to Use Agents.—By the use of agents instead of dealers for distribution the exporter places at least one intermediary between himself and his ultimate distributors. He must do this, as a rule, because his line, through style change or price fluctuation, must be ordered in small quantities, and often an agent is necessary to attend to the wants of the dealer, where jobbers or wholesalers will not stock the goods. To select and call on these agents periodically, a traveling representative of the exporter is desirable, though not essential.

Selecting the Market.—A world-wide campaign is seldom necessary or desirable at the start. Markets showing the most likely sales possibilities should be selected and tried out first, perhaps one or two at a time. The final selection is a matter of individual judgment, although export agencies exist to assist the manufacturer or exporter who is not fully equipped to make his own decisions. By going slowly at first, less likelihood of error exists.

Planning the Advertising Campaign.—No sales campaign can be successful without a certain amount of advertising. American products have gained a foothold abroad largely through advertising. Export advertising agencies, evolving from space brokers for foreign publications, have now come to serve exporters most effectively in providing intelligent service at the minimum cost to the advertiser. The most successful of these have applied American methods of merchandising and advertising through associate agencies abroad. In this way the foreign "flavor" has been added to the effective "pull" of the American advertisement. Another method is where the manufacturer permits his foreign sales agent the expenditure of his advertising appropriation. This method has its disadvantages and is being rapidly discarded by progressive exporters.

Under the first, or "centralized control," method the American advertising agency plans the world-wide advertising campaign; sets up appropriations for each market; selects the foreign media and devises schedules for each media; creates the advertisements in the American office and sends them to the foreign distributors for approval; and in every way controls the advertisement from its creation to its final appearance in the foreign publication. The associate agency abroad consults freely with the sales agency of the exporter, learns the peculiarities of the product and the selling angles, and supplies the home agency with market data for the compilation of budgets. The local distributor abroad furnishes the associate agency with an accurate picture of what is to be accomplished from the sales angle. When the advertisement has been created in the home agency it is sent to the associate agency abroad and translated, and all the local details are handled by the associate agency. Schedule of insertion dates, however, is kept under the control of the home agency, although subject to change for good reasons arising out of special conditions.

How to Reach Foreign Dealers.—The selling effort exercised by the dealer abroad is largely dependent upon the demand from the consumer. Substitution is an evil abroad, however, just as it is at home. The foreign product is at a disadvantage when competing with foreign products behind their own tariff walls. It is the quality appeal, in most instances, that makes the imported product attractive, especially when a local product is manufactured under tariff protection. The only free markets, where products of all nations compete on an absolutely even basis, are those where raw materials form the overwhelming background of livelihood. Here dealers are governed chiefly by price and only secondly by the volume of business they can do or the quality.

Profits and Sales.—A dealer is attracted by a product chiefly because of its sales value and the resulting profit he can make out of it. The discount to the dealer is of paramount importance if the product is at all saleable. First, therefore, the price must be right, then the quality equal to that of the competitor. In essentially price markets quality appeals but little, for purchasing power is the governing factor. No matter what inducements in the form of discounts are offered a dealer, therefore, in such markets, he will not handle a product that is out of line in price, simply because he cannot sell it.

Dealer Financing.—Many foreign dealers are so closely tied up with local jobbers and wholesalers that they cannot afford to stock a line that involves a cash outlay. Terms of payment then become the selling argument. It is not wise for a manufacturer or exporter, however, to finance a dealer. This should be left to local banks. These institutions know the local dealers' credit and if it is sound will guarantee his account or arrange for payment in some other way.

Goods that Can Be Sold Direct.—There are many classes of goods that can be sold direct to dealers among the staples that change little in style and price. Builders' supplies, household utensils and hardware, office supplies, watches, cheap jewelry, clocks, fountain pens, flashlights, fire-extinguishers, and like products, all fall within this category. Motor accessories can be easily sold direct to garages and motor-car dealers abroad. The test lies in their staple quality.

The Middleman Abroad.—The foreign jobbers and wholesalers naturally intervene between American exporters and foreign dealers, especially where the dealer must have credit. They are also essential where transportation or banking difficulties entail a separate distributing organization.

Dealers Types and How to Reach Them.—Dealers abroad group themselves naturally by the commodities in which they specialize. The most common shops found in most foreign cities are drug and pharmaceutical shops, hardware stores, drygoods stores, grocery stores, furniture stores, and haberdashers. Then there are department stores in most foreign cities of any size. As towns decrease in size, the tendency toward specialization disappears until in villages and very small towns the general store is the rule. These dealers, if they are to be reached by mail, must have a catalogue in the language they can read, which is usually not English nor even Spanish, although many millions of people in the world use both languages. The illustrations must be profuse, as they mean more to the average foreign dealer than reading matter. Finally, the prices quoted should include cost, insurance, and freight to the nearest port.

Consumer Demand.—First attract the foreign consumer's interest. This is not difficult as a rule, especially with people of an uneducated type. Little is accomplished by the negative appeal or the "knock" to the competitor's goods abroad. The positive appeal that gives a reason or implies a benefit is generally the most successful. Such appeal as a rule can only be broadcast through intelligent advertising. So educated has the average foreign dealer become to American selling methods, that he now asks immediately, "How much advertising are you willing to do?" He knows that consumer demand bears a direct relation to advertising. Advertising is also the great bane of the substitutor. If the consumer learns to know a product by its trademark or "chop," as it is called in China, great difficulty is experienced by those who would induce him to take a substitute.

Coordination of Advertising and Sales.—The advertising campaign must of course be carefully coordinated with sales effort. The dealers should stock the goods before the campaign is put on, so that its value will not be affected by lost sales. Such coordination is more easily accomplished through experienced advertising agencies than in any other way. It is to the dealer's interest to have the goods on hand when the campaign for the consumer's interest is started.

Foreign Mail Orders.—Foreign mail-order business has developed to important proportions in recent years. Inaccessible regions such as the interiors of Brazil, Colombia, Venezuela, China, etc., have proven a boon to the mail-order house. Special types of goods not easily obtained from local dealers form the principal commodities included in these mail-order catalogues, which are sent in appropriate languages to many parts of the world.

The Factory Representative.—The factory representative should be primarily a missionary salesman. He should assume the rôle of teacher and attempt to impart to his dealer or agent clientele throughout the world the secret of successful sales methods at home. He should not be expected to sell or to show any appreciable results during his stay in a given territory. It is the results that come as an aftermath to his visit in the *sustained* increase in sales that show whether he has done his job well. The cost of sending a first-rate factory representative on such a mission is small compared with the results that can be obtained. The factory representative is most useful where sales are spotty in various foreign territories. Such conditions, as a rule, portend faulty sales organization, and the help of a capable factory-trained salesman is often the needed panacea.

How a Factory Representative Functions.—

Whether the factory representative should travel extensively or devote his time to intensive development is often a matter of existing organization problems. Trips to appoint new agents can often be more hurried and more extensive than those taken to bolster up old agencies. The problem may be one of elimination of a top-heavy sales organization abroad. In either of the last two instances considerable time may be required. Above all, the factory representative should be liberal-minded and not a devotee to the rule of thumb.

Different territories may require different adaptations of home sales methods, and the ideal traveler for a manufacturer is one who recognizes these differences and lays his plans accordingly. He can be greatly fortified in a preliminary way and much time and expense saved if the territory, its possibilities and potentialities, is fairly accurately surveyed before he leaves. Otherwise he may be sent to do the impossible. Basic information is readily available at home to show the manufacturer and his traveling representative what the territory through which he expects to travel is capable of producing in sales.

The Representative's Way Should Be Prepared.—Little is gained, as a rule, by surprise visits by a sales representative to his foreign agents. As a matter of fact, warning of such visits often tends to correct some of the faults that are apparent from sales reports. The good agent welcomes the factory representative. Much preparatory work can be done by circularizing lists of dealers or agents of the representative's coming if he be sent to appoint new agents or dealers. The company and its products are then known to the dealer or agent when the factory representative approaches them. The trade press abroad can be used to good advantage toward the same end. This is especially true of highly organized markets such as the British, Canadian, and German. Export trade journals published in the United States and read extensively abroad for their technical information are excellent media for this purpose.

House Organ and Catalogues.—The house organ is often used not wisely but too well. Material designed primarily for domestic salesmen is not always adapted to the needs of foreign sales forces. The best solution is an overseas edition in appropriate language designed and contributed to principally by foreign dealers, agents, or branches. Catalogues, of course, should always be in the appropriate commercial language of the area to which they are sent, and prices listed separately.

Agent or Dealer?—What the manufacturer does at home in the matter of distributing his goods is often a fairly good criterion of what he should do abroad. Some things are absolutely taboo both at home and abroad; for example, appointment of a dealer as agent and expecting him to obtain business from other dealers. The product determines largely the method of distribution, and when a method is determined upon it should be made standard for a given sales territory and not combined with other types of distribution.

Dealers Are Not Salesmen.—Dealers stock goods and display them. The sales driving force must come from direct-to-consumer advertising or from the local sales agent. Thus, standard products needing little salesmanship are ideal products for dealer distribution. A dealer may be converted into an agent by displaying or developing sales talent, but then his status should be definitely changed and he should not be allowed to distribute to the consumer direct.

Manufacturer's Agent the Sales Crusader.—Overcoming sales resistance, working up selling appeal, and planning distribution are the function of the manufacturer's agent. He must teach the consumer to like a given product and to use it. Products which should be distributed through manufacturers' agents are not the self-sellers. They are things that need to be sold, and require the personal supervision of an agent on the spot to help sell them.

Profit-Sharing vs. Sales Incentive.—One thing that may convert a dealer into an agent is greater profit. He may turn salesman if the inducement is great enough. A small dealer who is successful in a small area, even though his sales are large, is not necessarily fitted to be a sole agent for a larger territory. In some territories dealers perform the function of dealer and wholesaler or jobber separately, but do not attempt to sell other local dealers. Their wholesale and jobbing functions are reserved for inland or up-country territories. In fixing trade discounts, competitors prices, easily obtained as a rule, are essential in order that net prices may not be far out of line with those of competitive goods of equal quality.

Consumer Appeal.—The consumer must be sold first. Before merit, before price, or before profit the dealer places consumer demand. With the almost universal disappearance of retail salesmanship advertising has had to supply the appeal to the consumer. A million people can be reached by a strong pulling advertisement, whereas a hundred could possibly not be reached in a year by a persuasive retail salesman. With the consumer appeal must go a well-organized dealer distribution, or its effect is lost. Consumer appeal to a market without purchasing power is often misspent energy, and ill-timed appeal, taking no consideration of buying seasons, is largely vitiated. If the dealer is stocked with the product, therefore, in time for the buying season, and then the appeal is made to the consumer, the results are usually satisfactory.

Local Advertising Has Its Advantages and Drawbacks.—The greatest argument against the use of the local advertising agency is the waste. Economy in art work, cuts, and other charges is effected through mass production at a given central point. Local feeling and color can be added through associate agencies. One man or set of men should direct the copy appeal for the entire world-wide advertising campaign, according to one school of thought. Another school takes violent exception and says that foreign advertising antagonizes the sensibilities of a local community.

Foreign Branches.—After an agent has built up his principal's business abroad he should not be thrown over and a branch established, because of the saving that can be effected. He may resent this and cause trouble and loss to the manufacturer. If erstwhile agents can be given some part in the new branch organization it nearly always pays. Either as branch manager or principal distributor an ex-agent is often successful, especially if some of the old profit-sharing incentive is retained in his new rôle. The quota system or bonus system as a rule operates as successfully throughout the world as it does at home.

Should Branch Managers Control Advertising?—The branch manager is a salesman and not an advertising man. In attempting to control advertising locally he is open to the same criticism as holds true with the agent, and in advertising costs he cannot compete with the central advertising agency. Many ludicrous mistakes have been made by American advertising agencies in not consulting more freely with branch managers of their clients. The branch manager or factory representative can often supply valuable data to the American advertising agency scarcely obtainable in any other way.

Conclusion.—Advertising and selling abroad, while differing in method and in some cases in technique from domestic advertising and selling, is in principle remarkably similar. The extension of American sales methods abroad through centralized control has long proven successful. The same is true of advertising through the central agency with associates abroad. The two activities are closely allied and should be carefully coordinated for the greatest success.

APPENDICES

Some Successful Campaigns Abroad

APPENDIX I

"Old Man Oats"

More people in more countries eat Quaker Oats than any other packaged food product. The policies underlying the foreign advertising of what is perhaps the world's best-known food should, therefore, interest the student of export affairs.

It has taken forty years to achieve the commanding position this distinctively American trademarked food now occupies. A world-wide sales organization has been supported by millions of dollars in advertising, placed in every country where there are printing facilities for the language.

The advertising of Quaker Oats is centralized through National Export Advertising Service, Inc., New York. Campaigns are prepared in some twenty-seven languages and are read by forty-four nations. All basic copy is in English and is controlled directly by the head office of the Quaker Oats Company in Chicago. Every line is edited and approved by an authority on dietetics. Quaker Oats permit no exaggerated statements nor any capable misconstruction. Such a policy may appear overly careful in these days of high-pressure advertising, but the expanding world sales of this product—its continued dominance of the market—are striking proof that strict truth pays in the long run.

From the start, Quaker Oats was greatly handicapped in foreign markets. It was a breakfast food. Yet almost nowhere could it be sold as such. People do not eat hearty breakfasts in many countries. To this day Quaker Oats is not sold, nor advertised, as a breakfast food. It is marketed as a health food and used in a variety of ways practically unknown to consumers in this country. The adaptation of the general health appeal to local conditions in various countries is the secret and success of Quaker Oats advertising.

No effort is ever made to translate or to make more understandable the logotype "Quaker Oats." To many people it is merely a collection of phonetic characters. In Arabic, it is a sound, "Kwacher oatch"; to the Latin American it is: "Quaker"; to the Chinese, it is "Old Man Oats."

But understandable or not, that name, sound, or chop is indelibly fixed in the minds of millions of consumers. It represents a certain kind of food, and substitutes, even though they may be relatively good and possibly less expensive, are not readily accepted; nor will they be until they, too, create their own market.

To localize Quaker Oats advertising still further native illustrations are used in many countries. These follow in the main the central theme chosen for all campaigns, differing merely in artistic treatment, costuming, and the racial characteristics of the figures illustrated.

The press advertising is carried in newspapers and

magazines principally, although store display material and health booklets are widely distributed to assist in carrying the message to the consumer. Demonstrations are carried in many countries to supplement the educational program, especially in countries where the masses are more or less illiterate and press advertising would be inefficient.

The package itself is one of the most valuable advertising media for Quaker Oats. The company believes that the ideal export label should tell the people of the world, in their own language, what is inside the tin, what the product is for and how it should be used. The label has undergone a period of development from the unsatisfactory gummed label to the present label lithographed on the tin itself, and printed in as many as fifty-seven different languages or dialects.

Quaker Oats is among the pioneers of foreign advertising. There is no means of measuring today the immense value to the company of its world-wide goodwill. There is little doubt that its future export business will continue to be highly profitable.

زیادہ طاقت انسان کو بہادر بناتی ہے
طاقت خوراک سے آتی ہے۔ کھیلوں۔ کاروبار اور سکول میں بازی لے جانے
کے لئے کوئکر اوٹس کھائیے۔ جو کہ طاقت سے بھرپور ہے۔
کوئکر اوٹس میں 65 فیصدی طاقت بخش اجزا اور 16 فیصدی پٹھے بنانے والی پروٹین
ہے۔ اس میں خون اور اعصاب بنانے والے وٹامن اور معدنی مادے بھی ہیں اور اسکا چھان ہم ہے
ہر روز کوئکر اوٹس کھائیے۔ اپنے آپ کو بہتر محسوس کیجئے اور خوب کام کیجئے۔
کوئکر اوٹس آسانی سے تیار کئے جانے کے علاوہ سستا بھی ہے۔
کوئکر اوٹس
Quaker Oats
انسانی ہاتھوں کے چھوئے بغیر بنتا ہے

哥哥弟弟上學去

凡屬智慧之父母每日早晨均用麥片養育其兒童因麥片爲特別補助氣力之良方又能驅除兒童在學校工作之疲乏並能供給各種之補質使兒童成爲强壯發育完全蓋麥片中亦含有一種似菓乾之粉有助補各機關之可能請各家庭用此種滋補麥片爲食品是種麥片未經人手接觸之也

966

Quaker Oats

ESTE QUADRO MOSTRA A IMPORTANCIA DO PRIMEIRO ALMOÇO

O mappa abaixo é baseado em pesquisas scientificas realisadas por uma das mais notaveis universidades do mundo.

A linha pontuada indica a energia derivada de uma primeira refeição leve e inadequada. A linha carregada mostra a quantidade de energia derivada de uma primeira refeição correctamente equilibrada.

O espaço entre as duas linhas é uma indicação bastante exacta da differença entre o homem que segue para a frente e o que fica atraz-a creança que é um alumno laureado e a que é designada como "atrazada."

Sem sufficiente energia não podemos fazer o nosso melhor trabalho; não podemos pensar tão claramente, não estamos tão activos, fatigamo-nos rapidamente. É então logico perguntar como poderemos augmentar a nossa energia e assim trabalhar melhor, pensar melhor, avançar mais rapidamente.

A resposta é simples. Comer alimentos que produzam energia. Quaker Oats é um dos alimentos conhecidos que produz mais energia. Convem tomal-o todos os dias, á primeira refeição. É surprehendente como este alimento nos faz sentir melhor, nos põe mais bem dispostos, como a nossa mente se torna mais activa, quanto o nosso trabalho melhora.

Muito do nosso trabalho, de facto 70%, é feito na manhã. É por isso que temos necessidade de uma primeira refeição restauradora e bem equilibrada de Quaker Oats todos os dias.

9A.M. 10A.M. 11A.M. 12M. 1P.M.

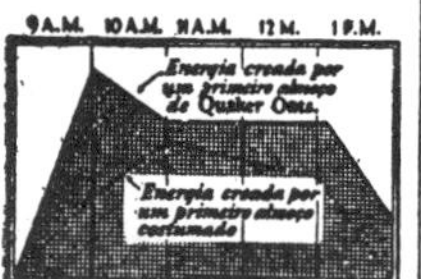

Para a escola . . .

OS paes sensatos animam os seus filhos a comer Quaker Oats todas as manhãs.

Dá-lhes superabundancia de energia. Fortifica-os contra a fadiga duante as horas da manhã, quando o trabalho escolar é mais custoso. Fornece-lhes com fartura os verdadeiros elementos exigidos pela natureza para um desenvolvimento forte e resistente.

Quaker Oats tem um delicioso sabor de nozes, apreciado por milhões de pessoas em todo o mundo. Sirva-se Quaker Oats todos os dias. É um alimento saudavel e nutritivo para toda a familia.

Quaker Oats

2658A

APPENDIX II

From Bathtubs to Automobiles

Not so long ago, and even today to a certain extent, European cities were full of tiny automobiles affectionately known as "bathtubs" because of the marked resemblance which they bore to that common household appliance. They held two people—uncomfortably—but were the last word in inexpensive transportation.

At about this time an American manufacturer of inexpensive automobiles who had been selling his product in Europe for several years appointed the European branches of an American advertising agency, Erwin, Wasey & Company, to prepare and place his advertising in Europe. He furnished the agency with a list of selling-points of his product—economy, beauty, durability and all the other qualities which most automobile manufacturers were at that time claiming for their cars. Advertising cleverly built around these points would doubtless have sold a respectable quota of this particular brand of automobile, but the agency cast about for some more unusual appeal.

They found this in the limited capacity of the inexpensive "bathtub" type of vehicle which was the chief competitor of the American car. The first appeal was to the European's love of his family. Consequently the opening advertisement in the campaign showed a picture of a nurse and three children looking forlornly off at the parents who were driving away for an outing in their tiny automobile. The headline, in French, read *"N'oubliez pas les enfants"* ("Don't forget the children"). And the copy went on to explain that it was not necessary to leave the children at home when the family went for a drive—that there was one inexpensive car large enough to carry the whole family. The second piece of copy was captioned *"La Dimanche des ecoliers"* ("The Sunday of the school children"). It further elaborated on the theme suggested in the first advertisement, and suggested that the children of the family should be given the opportunity of getting out into the country even before the parents. It showed how, with this more capacious car, this was now possible even for families with a limited income.

This fresh theme in automobile advertising not only resulted in a very gratifying increase in the sale of the particular car, but also created a lively interest in motoring as a healthful pastime for the whole family rather than for the heads of the family alone.

APPENDIX III

They Had to Sell Refrigeration Before They Could Sell Refrigerators in Europe

In the early days of the past decade, a well-known American manufacturer of electric refrigerators decided to enter the European market. He established his first contacts in France and, having put his business on a working basis, undertook an advertising campaign to bring his product to the attention of the public. The Paris office of Erwin, Wasey & Company was intrusted with the preparation and placing of the advertising.

A logical method of procedure might have been to study the advertising of the company which was then appearing in the United States and to translate and adapt this to the French market. Copy would have proclaimed the advantages of this company's product as against competitive refrigerators. It would have taken for granted the fact that the old type of refrigerator was in use in most French homes. It would have attempted to convince the people that it was the part of good judgment to substitute modern electric refrigeration for the obsolete ice-box. And the campaign would have died on its feet.

Instead of following this line of least resistance, however, a careful survey of the market was made and it was found that even the old type of ice-box refrigeration was almost unknown in France. As in most other European countries, the only known refrigerators were dark corners and cool cellars. It was immediately obvious that the American company would have first of all to teach the people of France the advantages of scientific refrigeration before they could hope to sell their own advanced method of preserving foods. A campaign designed to accomplish this was at once prepared.

The first piece of copy started off—"*Ca Vous Etonnera*" ("It Will Amaze You")—and then went on to explain in a simple, interesting manner, the extraordinary advantages of clean, dry, iceless refrigeration. Repeated emphasis of simple health facts which, in America, are taken for granted gradually succeeded in creating in the minds of the French public a desire for just the type of refrigeration which this company had for sale. As a result the use of modern refrigerators has become more and more common and the company which pioneered in the field is reaping dividends in the form of very substantial sales of their product. They are today established not only in France, but in England, Germany, Belgium, Holland, Switzerland, Spain, Italy, and even in the cold northern countries of Sweden, Finland, Denmark and Norway. In all of these countries ignorance regarding modern methods of refrigeration had to be overcome before sales were possible.

Without careful consideration of the habits of their potential consumers, the success of this company

Des *Millions* de gourmets savourent chez eux des boissons rafraîchies par plus d'un *Million* de Frigidaire

COLDER
OFF
COLD CONTROL

Pour la preparation des entremets

Chaque Frigidaire domestique est muni d'un perfectionnement exclusif qui en augmente considérablement la valeur. Il s'agit du nouveau "Cold Control" qui permet d'accélérer la congélation dans les tiroirs.

Tout appareil réfrigérateur qui ne porte pas cette plaque n'est pas un Frigidaire.

PLUS de 1.300.000 familles possèdent aujourd'hui leur Frigidaire. Etant donné que les bienfaits de ce merveilleux réfrigérateur électrique automatique profitent à tous les habitants du foyer, à combien faudrait-il chiffrer le nombre de gens qui ignoraient le délice de boire frais et qui, maintenant, savourent chez eux les vins bien rafraichis, les boissons glacées bien préparées sans se donner d'autre peine que de retirer du tiroir de leur Frigidaire le cube de glace fait au calibre de leur verre? A ce plaisir, ils ajoutent les économies, l'hygiène qu'un Frigidaire assure du fait de son fonctionnement irréprochable, de son "service" parfait, des garanties sans pareilles qu'offre le patronage de la General Motors. Comment s'étonner dès lors que Frigidaire soit le réfrigérateur électrique le plus vendu? Seul Frigidaire est fabriqué par la General Motors. Méfiez-vous des imitations. Agences Frigidaire dans les principales villes de France.

Tous les modèles Frigidaire peuvent être achetés à crédit dans les meilleures conditions.

must surely have been far less rapid and far less extensive than it has been.

It is seldom safe, in considering Europe as a market for American products, to take as a criterion upon which to base advertising and merchandising plans the contemporary American attitude toward these products.

APPENDIX IV

"A Skin You Love to Touch"

"Beauty has a universal appeal. Every woman wants—and all men admire—a beautiful skin; hence the slogan 'A skin you love to touch' creates an instinctive desire in women and a subtle appeal in men.

"Now, all women can not possess beautiful features, but nearly all can have a clean, healthy, glowing complexion, in truth a skin one loves to touch. Proper care of the skin and the daily use of Woodbury Facial Soap will safeguard the skin from the ravages of wind, dust, and sun, prevent clogging of the pores, and enable most women to keep a pure, vigorous complexion, free from impurities and ugly blemishes."

This is the message, in substance, that Woodbury advertising has been carrying year after year to women in Cuba, Porto Rico, and other countries through the Gotham Advertising Agency of New York.

Woodbury's Facial is a quality soap. It is not merely a fine toilet soap, but the basic element of a skin treatment. To popularize this treatment and drive home the necessity of taking daily care of the skin has been the principal objective of Woodbury advertising.

The cost of a cake of soap is within the potential reach of all users of soaps, but we know that in Cuba, Porto Rico, and other countries the price automatically confines the sale of Woodbury to a limited class. For this reason Woodbury advertising in those countries has been directed exclusively to the woman of cultivated tastes, who, by training and environment, is accustomed to the best things and can afford to indulge her preferences.

In other words, Woodbury has been advertised in overseas countries as a treatment to purify and beautify the skin of the better classes of women. Our copy and illustration are addressed to these women. And, contrary to popular belief, smart society women in Cuba, Porto Rico, and other countries dress and live very much like those in any other country except for some typical affectations which are an inheritance from the times when *la mantilla* was in flower. They have their preferences too in the type of magazine and newspaper they read—which are precisely the same magazines and newspapers used in the advertising of Woodbury's Facial Soap.

APPENDIX V

A Labor Lightener with Universal Appeal

An outstanding American concern whose product and advertising have penetrated every civilized country of the globe is the 3-in-One Oil Company. One of the most successful advertising campaigns this company recently has run is the one in support of its merchandising and sales-promotion work in the British Isles. This advertising plan for 3-in-One Oil has been based upon a carefully outlined space campaign, backed up solidly by dealer-help material.

Some examples of typical copy now being run are reproduced herewith through the courtesy of the Gotham Advertising Agency of New York. These advertisements appear in a wide selection of publications, embracing many of the London national dailies, local newspapers, general and women's magazines, and trade journals.

The advertising, whether to consumer or trade, stresses the superiority of 3-in-One over all other packaged oils. It points out the care which has been taken to have and keep the ingredients 100 per cent pure and to so select and combine these ingredients as consistently to produce those remarkable results which have made 3-in-One Oil so justly popular during the thirty-five years it has been on the market.

ES un proceso natural, sin dolor, tan bien regularizado como las funciones de todos los órganos de nuestro cuerpo. La vieja epidermis se desprende y otra piel nueva viene a reponerla. El conocimiento de este proceso ha hecho que muchas mujeres de belleza ordinaria se transformen en bellezas de irresistible encanto.

Cuide debidamente la nueva piel y verá usted cuan limpia, suave y vigorosa se pondrá. El tratamiento del Jabón Facial Woodbury es lo único que se requiere.

Conserve el cútis libre de granos, espinillas, manchas e impurezas. Durante el día la piel absorbe los vapores nocivos y gérmenes que flotan en la atmósfera; el sol y el viento contribuyen su dañina influencia, se pone áspera la piel, los poros se llenan de estas impurezas, y el resultado es una tez grasienta y malsana.

El Jabón Facial Woodbury sólo requiere quince minutos diarios para conservar el cútis limpio y saludable. Comience esta noche antes de retirarse. Observe entonces la nueva salud de su piel, su vigorosidad y encanto.

Expuesto en los principales establecimientos de las Filipinas

Agentes BEHN, MEYER & CO., H. MIJ.
P. O. BOX 298 MANILA
CEBU - ILOILO

Para conservar la salud de la piel y para la toilette en general, use

JABÓN FACIAL WOODBURY

La mayoría de las afecciones cutáneas obedecen a los poros tapados. Conserve los poros limpios.

The advertising in the daily and weekly newspapers features the essential and uniquely advantageous properties of 3-in-One Oil in house, shop, and garage, indoors and outdoors, for lubrication, prevention of rust, and cleaning and polishing.

The advertisements in the women's magazines call particular attention to the multiplicity of the uses of 3-in-One Oil in and about the house, its advantages as a labor lightener and saver, and its general handiness.

Advertisements in the trade publications emphasize 3-in-One as one of the fastest movers and quickest return sale and turnover items purchaseable and call attention to the fact that, beyond any other article of its kind, its stocking and sale are, and always have been, supported by generous, widespread consumer advertising and an extremely liberal dissemination of dealer help and display material.

The broadside shown has been widely distributed among dealers and factors. In addition to this broadside, dealers throughout the British Isles have been supplied with various booklets and brochures emphasizing the uses and merits of 3-in-One Oil, together with a very attractive transparency, as well as display cards and window material suited to the various trades.

Lighten your housework

Clean and polish the 3-in-One way.

Try this new and easy housework aid. So easy and pleasing. A yard or two of cheese cloth or soft material, sprinkled with a few drops of Three-in-One Oil and rolled up until well permeated, makes a dust collecting duster, which relegates the dust scattering method of the past to where it belongs.

3-in-One

Prevents Rust - OILS - *Cleans & Polishes*

Three-in-One is the best oil for all lubricating purposes too. For your machine, vacuum cleaner, gramophone and lawn mower. Stops hinges from squeaking, and prevents rust on stoves, etc. Three-in-One is the ideal household oil.

Sold by all Grocers, Ironmongers, Stores, Chemists, Cycle Dealers, Sports Outfitters. In ***9d., 1/6*** *and* ***3/-*** *bottles and* ***1/6*** *Handy cans.*

Also the new **OILRIGHT CAN, 9d.**

FREE. Test this new dusting method at our expense. Those mentioning "Home Magazine" can have a generous free sample, together with a Dictionary of Uses. Send to:—

THREE-IN-ONE OIL CO.
(Dept. H.M.)
4 & 5, Stonecutter St., London, E.C.4

APPENDIX VI

"Horlick's for Sleep"

An unusually clear-cut example of a successful advertising campaign growing out of facts revealed by a field investigation is the Horlick's Malted Milk campaign in England.

When the account was taken over by the J. Walter Thompson Company, no one was able to say what the product was most used for. It had been advertised over a long period of years for every conceivable use. Most of the advertisements had offered it in very general terms as a drink to keep all members of the family well and fit. Horlick's is much less a soda-fountain drink in England than in America, and much more a home drink. A large business had been built up in this way, but it was threatened by a competing product which cost less.

A consumer investigation uncovered the fact that an overwhelming number of the people who took Horlick's or any similar drink did so last thing at night, and a surprising proportion of these said that they took it to help them sleep, the others for the most part being unable to give a specific reason. This pointed to the advisability of concentrating the advertising on one specific use for the product—as a bed-time drink to induce sleep. But a further field study was made to determine more closely how large the potential market was for this use. This investigation showed that seventy per cent of the people in England either suffer from actual wakefulness at night or interrupted rest, or wake in the morning feeling fatigued. This fact left no misgivings in the minds of those in charge of the advertising, and the "sleep" campaign was launched.

But Horlick's was an old product. To capture public attention, it was important to do more than merely shout "Horlick's for sleep." To inject news into the campaign, therefore, and to establish the Horlick company as an authority on great matters, the campaign announced the interesting and quickly believable fact that "sound sleep is more important than long sleep." This statement, expressed in various ways, was supported by evidence supplied from medical sources. Convincing use was made of charts of laboratory tests relative to sleep supplied by Dr. Donald Laird, coauthor of the recent book entitled *Sleep*.

Each advertisement, of course, came round, in a logical manner, to Horlick's as the means of insuring sound sleep.

The sales figures are confidential, but it can be said that this campaign has been strikingly successful.

"SLEEP has not only *length* but *depth*"

says an eminent scientist

It is not only how *long* we sleep that counts but how *soundly*. Actually 70 out of 100 people living in modern towns are getting insufficient rest!

NAPOLEON is said to have slept only 5 hours at a stretch — John Wesley compromised with 6 hours . . . one of the most famous scientific inventors of the modern age takes his rest in a series of brief naps at any hour of the day . . .

How is it possible, one asks, for such active brains to obtain sufficient rest in such short periods? And the answer is — to quote the words of a well-known authority — "sleep has not only length but *depth*."

Deep sleep alone is truly refreshing. A few hours' profound, peaceful slumber are worth more than many hours of wakeful tossing.

Yet deep sleep is what many of us fail to get. Worry, overwork, too little fresh air, tend to make us wakeful. Cold, or slight indigestion, prevents us from sleeping as soundly as we should.

That is why active men and women need Horlick's—a hot cupful every night at bedtime! It is a splendid way to ensure sound, natural sleep.

Horlick's is made from fresh, creamy milk, wheat, and malted barley. It is extremely nourishing, yet so digestible that even a baby can readily assimilate it.

As you sip the tempting cupful, its nourishing warmth penetrates your whole system. Tense, weary nerves relax. Your digestion gets to work . . . gently, soothingly . . . you feel satisfied, nourished, in the mood for sleep. And when you sleep you sleep soundly. No digestive disturbances —no spasms of chilliness or hunger disturb your rest!

Start taking Horlick's today! Mix your drink with the special Horlick's Mixer, which makes it doubly smooth and delicious. Chemists and grocers have Horlick's, in sealed glass bottles in four sizes.

CHART showing two types of curve illustrating depth of sleep. The majority of people sleep most deeply at the end of the second hour — their sleep gradually diminishing in depth till about the 8th hour. These people on the whole work best early in the day. The second, and less usual type of curve (dotted), belongs to the sleeper who has two "maximum depth" points during the night — one about the end of the third hour and one shortly before the normal waking time. Such people frequently are sleepy in the morning.

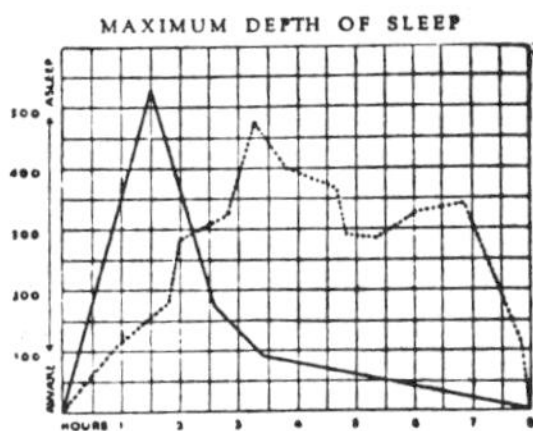

HORLICK'S

PLAIN OR CHOCOLATE FLAVOURED

8450—R Horlick's Glasgow Bulletin 11 Feb. 1930 11 x 6½
Daily Mirror 14 ,,
Sunday Pictorial 9 March
Daily Sketch 12 ,,

APPENDIX VII

A Winner on Points

In handling the advertising for the various cars of General Motors throughout the world the branch offices of the J. Walter Thompson Company put out campaigns locally which are suited to the conditions of the individual countries. At the same time these offices are frequently supplied with advertising and merchandising ideas from the Plan Board of the New York office which are universal in their scope and application.

An excellent example of this was the campaign developed for the Chevrolet Passenger Car designed to meet the competition of the cars against which this automobile sold, and at the same time to give the Chevrolet dealer a central peg on which he could hang all his merchandising efforts. This idea as originated in the New York office of the J. Walter Thompson Company was that the central feature of the campaign should be a Value Chart to visualize in dramatic form the advantages which the Chevrolet possessed over its competitors. The chart was presented in the form of a sort of voting ballot listing the ten most important features which the Chevrolet had as compared with its competitors, and the reader was asked to actually check off these points himself.

The same chart idea was to be carried into all forms of sales promotion and merchandising with a display of the chart in show windows, the use of actual small charts for distribution while giving demonstrations, the covering of each of the points by the salesman in his talk, etc.

This central idea was enthusiastically received not only by the central organization of the General Motors Export Company in New York, but by the plants abroad, and the adaptations of it that were made and the various forms in which it was presented to the public in the different parts of the world are indicated by the accompanying proofs.

This world-wide campaign represented the use of an idea so basically sound that it appealed to people everywhere and resulted in a unified world effort on this car to achieve a preconceived aim, which was definitely to acquaint the people of the world with the salient features of this car in a way that would be interesting and which could be capitalized throughout the selling organization of this company.

Ideado para a velocidade e trafico modernos

Competindo em comodidade, elegancia e facilidade de manejo com os carros de preço muito mais elevado

Experimente-o com a Tabela de Valorisação na mão e verifique os diferentes pontos, comparando-o com outros carros de baixo preço que conheça. O concessionário mais proximo oferece-lhe esta ocasião de apreciar o verdadeiro valor de Chevrolet.

TODO o mundo quer conduzir um carro com a potencia que lhe dá um motor de seis cilindros e a comodidade de um chassis baixo e comprido, montado sobre molas compridas e flexiveis.

O Chevrolet reune todas as condições dos carros grandes, dentro dos limites de todas as fortunas. Antes de converter o dinheiro que destine a comprar um automovel, peça ao concessionário a Tabela de Valorisação e compare as condições dêste carro com os restantes do mesmo preço e com muitos outros mais caros.

No trafico das povoações ou cidades, é êle o primeiro a arrancar, devido á bomba aceleradora, que facilita de forma surpreendente a reprise, assegurando-lhe os seus travões melhorados o completo dominio do carro. Qualquer concessionário lhe fará, com prazer, uma demonstração e lhe dará todas as explicações.

General Motors Peninsular, S. A.

Fabricado pela General Motors

CHEVROLET SEIS

APPENDIX VIII

Personalizing Graham-Paige

The automobile manufacturer whose advertising is shown here has been particularly successful in getting overseas business in a very short period of time. This company, splendidly organized and with an unusually fine field force, backed by a complete line offering a full choice of sixes and eights, in the short space of two years established itself firmly in overseas markets.

Advertising played no small part in this success. The main idea was to personalize the line. When one thought of Graham-Paige cars, it was desired that one should also think of the three Graham brothers. These men, with established reputations in America for achievement, honesty, and integrity of purpose, must be made as well known to the dealer and prospective buyer overseas as they are at home. While the Graham brothers were known abroad to the more influential business people, they were not yet connected in a personalized way with the cars. The Millsco Agency, in charge of Graham overseas advertising, put into effect the plan illustrated, simple, dignified, and effective. The shield with the three knights emblazoned thereon; portrayed allegorically strength and honor. The three signatures not only personalized the advertisement, but made it a signed statement by these men, who were personally vouching for every claim made for their cars.

The appeal was successful. Almost unrealized by the buying fraternity in overseas markets, the three Graham brothers became so associated with the line as to give it a decided advantage over many competitive makes. It was humanized. The thought of personal interest and pledge was clearly understood. It is interesting to note that the same idea and the same appeal met with equal success whether it was present in the soft *Gujarati* of India, the sturdy Dutch of the Low Countries, or the fluid Spanish of the South.

A Car For Test is at Your Disposal

A new Graham-Paige, equipped with four speeds forward, awaits your pleasure. Prove for yourself the benefits of this new motoring achievement—a real difference in performance, with all the luxury and refinement of detail that distinguish a truly fine motor car. What day and hour will suit you best?

Joseph B. Graham
Robert C. Graham
Ray A. Graham

Five chasses—sixes and eights—in 21 models, at prices within the reach of practically every car buyer. All models, except the 610, equipped with four speeds forward (two quiet high speeds)

GRAHAM-PAIGE

અજમાયશ માટે તમારી તહેનાત માં કાર તૈયાર છે

ચારે સ્પીડ ફોરવર્ડ" વાલી નવી ગ્રાહામ-પેજ કાર તમારી તહેનાતમાં હાજર છે. મોટર-હારોને લગની આ સફળતા એટલે કે એક ખરી ઉમદા કારને અગ્રસ્થાને લાવનાર સર્વ તરેહના આરામ આપની સઘવડો અને તેની હરેક તપસીલોમાં રહેલી ભવ્યતા સાથે કાર્ય શક્તિ માં સમાયલી ખરી વિશેષતા ની તમારા લાભાર્થે ખાતરી કરી જુઓ. આ અજમાયશ માટે આપને ક્યો સમય અનુકૂળ થશે?

Joseph B. Graham
Robert C. Graham
Ray A. Graham

પાંચ શાસીસો - છ અને આઠ સીલેન્ડરો - ૨૨ મોડલો, વાસ્તવઃ કિંમત હરેકને પોશાય તેવી. મોડલ ૬૧૦ સિવાય બધાને ચાર સ્પીડ ટ્રાન્સમીશન બેફિ શબ્જારે ચડપો હોયછે

GRAHAM-PAIGE

Een wagen voor een proefrit staat voor U gereed!

Een gloednieuwe Graham-Paige, uitgerust met vier voorwaartsche versnellingen, staat voor een proefrit voor U gereed. Eerst dan zult U de laatste creatie op motorgebied volkomen kunnen waardeeren. De nieuwe Graham-Paige praesteert meer dan andere auto's. De afwerking is, als bij elke werkelijke luxewagen, tot in het kleinste onderdeel verzorgd.

Joseph B. Graham
Robert C. Graham
Ray A Graham

EEN UITNOODIGING — In districten waar de Graham-Paige automobielen op het oogenblik niet voldoende vertegenwoordigd zijn, is er gelegenheid voor verantwoordelijke zakenmenschen, die geinteresseerd zijn in de buitengewone vooruitzichten welke deze nieuwe modellen aanbieden, om het verkooperecht te verkrijgen.

GRAHAM-PAIGE
INTERNATIONAL CORPORATION
DETROIT, MICHIGAN, U. S. A.

GRAHAM-PAIGE

Cuatro modelos con cuatro velocidades, las dos altas silenciosas.

Sedán Modelo 629 de cinco asientos, con caja de cuatro velocidades, cigüeñal de siete cojinetes y frenos hidráulicos en las cuatro ruedas.

La tan anhelada meta perseguida por los Ingenieros automovilistas

La serie completa de automóviles Graham-Paige de seis y ocho cilindros, comprende 21 estilos de carrocerías en 5 modelos de chasis, a precios al alcance de todas las fortunas.

Modelos Sedán desde pesetas 10.650.

El cambio de marcha Graham-Paige de 4 velocidades con las dos altas silenciosas, establece nuevas normas de funcionamiento automotriz. En las grandes velocidades, determina una gran potencia sin perjuicio de la acción uniforme y económica del coche; la aceleración es rápida, suave y silenciosa; facilita la subida de pendientes pronunciadas y el funcionamiento del coche es perfecto sobre terreno llano. Hay un automóvil dispuesto para que usted mismo lo pruebe.

Joseph B. Graham
Robert C. Graham
Ray A. Graham

A. S. E. (S. A.)

Alcalá, 69 MADRID — P.º de Gracia, 28 BARCELONA

GRAHAM-PAIGE

APPENDIX IX

A Cuban "Home Run"

This is an interesting example of advertising that ties-up with a current local condition. Cubans are enthusiastic baseball fans, and the Millsco Agency, taking advantage of a long winning streak of a certain club, and knowing that the Cuban public were interested in this club particularly—as a popular native player had recently joined it and was responsible in large part for its success—used the familiar cartoon idea to increase the sale of a popular product. Cubans like cartoons, and the copy itself sells the idea in the latest Cuban baseball slang. Witness the use of the word "jonron" (pronounced "hone-rone"), which is nothing less than the Cuban conception of our familiar friend—the "home run."

A free translation of the advertisement follows:

Two famous products of Brooklyn—the baseball club and Gem Safety Razor Blades. . . . First fan "Sure thing, Bo, a change makes a big difference. Now just look at Brooklyn." Second fan, "Yeah,—and look at Gem Blades! I changed to 'em this morning and knocked the old beard for a home run with three on the bags. Shave with a Gem and your face never gets sore. Yeah, a change works wonders—why don't you change to Gem?"

2 FAMOSOS PRODUCTOS DE BROOKLYN—

el Club de BASEBALL

y HOJAS de FILO SUPERIOR GEM

Fanático No. 1: *"Está probado chico, un cambio oportuno es lo mejor. Fíjate en el Club de Brooklyn—"*

Fanático No. 2: *"¡Y en la hoja GEM! Cambié a ella esta mañana y le empujó un jonrón a mi barba con tres en bases. Aféitate con GEM y siempre tendrás la cara perfectamente limpia y fresca. Un cambio oportuno es lo mejor . . . cámbiate a la hoja GEM."*

American Safety Razor Corp., BROOKLYN, N. Y., E. U. A.

APPENDIX X

From Spain to China

There have been many arguments pro and con about the use of American copy overseas, but the fact remains that human emotions, in the main, are the same the world over, and if we get just the correct little local touches to American copy, it will make the sale in China just as easily as in Madrid.

Here is a case in point. The Millsco Agency, which has directed many successful export advertising campaigns for well-known American manufacturers, provides us a convincing example. The advertisement shown above, "A," certainly makes an interesting appeal to the average Occidental. Now look at "B," and you will see the force of the familiar human appeal. Millsco has trained its associate offices to follow the American copy closely; the policy must not be changed, for it is right; yet the associate has skillfully converted the ad into Chinese, holding the American layout, holding the American appeal, holding the American cleanness of arrangement and strong package display. Yet the Chinese reader has no unpleasant foreign reaction. The types of woman and child are familiar and correct. It is interesting to note that in China, where we have been told many things are topsy-turvy, the layout itself has been reversed, that the Chinese reader may start at the right and read downward, quite differently from his American cousin, who reads crosswise from left to right.

La Hora de Acostarse . . . es la Hora de Squibb

Protéjase en La Línea del Peligro donde la encía toca el diente

Cepíllese los Dientes para la Salud

LOS niños deben ser enseñados a cuidarse su dentadura. Cepillándolos diariamente con Crema Dental Squibb, los dientes se conservan sanos y vigorosos. La Crema Dental Squibb no solamente conserva los dientes blancos y limpios, sino que los protege científicamente contra la caries, pues contiene más de 50 por ciento de Leche de Magnesia Squibb, el medio más seguro y eficaz para neutralizar los ácidos que se forman en *La Línea del Peligro,* donde la encía toca el diente. La Crema Dental Squibb es eficaz, segura y agradable. Usela desde hoy en adelante y visite a su dentista dos veces al año.

E. R. SQUIBB & SONS, NUEVA YORK

Químicos Manufactureros Establecidos en el Año 1858

La Leche de Magnesia Squibb con que se prepara la Crema Dental Squibb es un producto puro y eficaz que no tiene el sabor terroso y desagradable de otros similares. Como antiácido y laxante suave no tiene igual.

須保護齒與齦相接處之危線

「齒貴保」牙膏中所含之「士貴寶」鎂汁，精純有效，毫無別種如土之惡味，其制酸及輕瀉助消之品質，亦爲別種所不及，

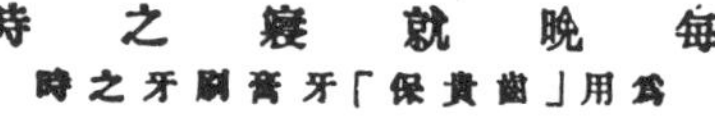

爲用「齒貴保」牙膏刷牙之時

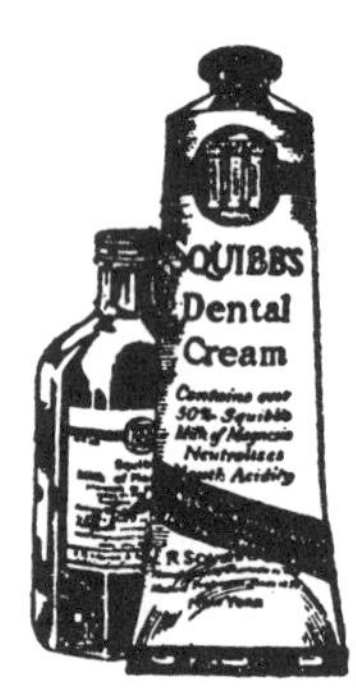

宜定時刷牙以維護健康

兒童須教以注意保護齒牙。日常用「齒貴保」牙膏以刷牙。則終其身齒牙可以健康强固。「齒貴保」牙膏對於齒牙，不但可使潔白。且有科學的保護力，使免腐朽。其成分中含有「士貴寶」鎂汁五成以上。此爲最安全最有效之制酸劑。功能滌除齒縫及危線處所積之口酸。「齒貴保」牙膏，安全無害。用之見效。請今日即購一管可也。

美國紐約

士貴寶父子化學公司製造

——創立於一八五八年

(二)

SQUIBB'S DENTAL CREAM

E. R. SQUIBB & SONS, NEW YORK

Manufacturing Chemists to the Medical Profession Since 1858

APPENDIX XI

ADVERTISING THROUGH THE PROFESSIONS

THE problem which confronts every export advertiser, of finding a copy theme of universal application has been solved in a most unique and unusual way by the Nash Motors Corporation in its 1930 series of advertisements released in countries abroad.

The basic thought involved is that throughout the world men respect the opinions of members of professional groups such as doctors, lawyers, artists, engineers.

These opinions are used to dramatize the Nash sales message. The headline of one advertisement reads, "The Doctor Speaks." Another says, "The Lawyer Speaks," and so throughout the series. The text gives details on why the man who is speaking prefers the Nash motor-car. It naturally rings true because it is written from the viewpoint of a specific individual. The copy is most readable, for it is of a conversational nature. There is complete avoidance of the superlatives so commonly associated with motor-car advertising.

The series brought favorable comment from dealers and agents in every part of the world and unusual reader interest regardless of language or latitude because of a copy subject intelligible and compelling to all mankind.

A secondary use also proved to be most important and helpful. It was found that these advertisements carried by salesmen and presented, in person, to prospects, opened the door to an interview and quickened the sale in remarkably efficient style.

For instance, salesmen calling on bankers would place the advertisements headed, "The Banker Speaks," before the prospect and ask for an opinion. It was found that in almost every instance the advertisement was read, if only for curiosity's sake. Again if the prospect happened to be an engineer, the advertisement which featured the engineer's point-of-view was used.

This series of Nash motor-car advertisements was released under the personal supervision of A. C. Peters, export sales promotion manager of the Nash Motors Corporation, in conjunction with the Dorland International Advertising Agency.

THE LAWYER SPEAKS!

"MERE eloquence, unsupported by facts, seldom wins a verdict in a court of law. ¶ We lawyers are trained to scrutinize the evidence submitted and to accept as facts only those contentions which can be definitely proven! ¶ I chose my motor car with an open mind and after a systematic study of the claims and counter claims of different manufacturers. ¶ In rendering a verdict in favor of a Nash "400" my judgment was swayed by the evidence of my own senses when its power, speed, and beauty were on trial, and by the testimony of owner friends as to its durability and low final cost. ¶ The confidence I placed in my Nash Twin-Ignition "8" when I bought it has been fully justified."

Notable Twin-Ignition Eight features include: *New Straight-Eight, Twin-Ignition Valve-in-head engine—9-bearing crankshaft—centralized chassis lubrication—Built-in automatic radiator shutters—hydraulic shock absorbers—Duplate non-shatterable plate glass throughout — steel spring covers with sealed-in lifetime lubrication*

(DEALER'S NAME)

THE AMBASSADOR SPEAKS!

"IT is a statesman's function to perceive promptly and to appraise fairly all trends which have become world wide.

"International acceptance of an idea or a product naturally influences the best minds of every nation.

"It does not surprise me to learn that in nineteen of the world's best markets the Nash "400" reigns supreme in its price field.

"I own a Nash myself and gladly acknowledge its many excellences.

"The recent purchase of Nash Twin Ignition "8's" by several royal families of Europe, who purchase only what pleases them, confirms my original belief that it is the peer of cars priced much higher."

Notable Twin-Ignition Eight features include: *New Straight-Eight, Twin-Ignition, Valve-in-head engine—9-bearing crankshaft—centralized chassis lubrication—Built-in automatic radiator shutters—hydraulic shock absorbers—Duplate non-shatterable plate glass throughout — steel spring covers with sealed-in lifetime lubrication*

(DEALER'S NAME)

NASH "400"

THE PLANTER SPEAKS!

"IN order to make my numerous tours of inspection, without interruption, over my large estates, I naturally need a car of dependability, power, comfort and economy.

"I find that my Nash '400' possesses all these attributes and many others. You may be sure it will continue to be my choice on account of its excellent performance record in my service.

"What I think of the Nash may be summed up in these few words—there are two cars on my plantation and they are both Nash Eights!"

Notable Twin-Ignition Eight features include: *New Straight-Eight, Twin-Ignition, Valve-in-head engine—9-bearing crankshaft—centralized chassis lubrication—Built-in automatic radiator shutters—hydraulic shock absorbers—Duplate non-shatterable plate glass throughout—steel spring covers with sealed-in lifetime lubrication.*

(DEALER'S NAME)

A WOMAN SPEAKS!

"I SUPPOSE every woman secretly hopes to own a car of her own some day—a car as personal as her jewels.

"No other gift ever meant so much to me as my new Twin-Ignition Nash "400" roadster. It is so trim and smart and easy to drive. Besides, I happen to be very fond of fresh air and sunshine.

"A roadster does seem like a selfish car, but when we can buy two Nashes for less than we paid for one big car, why shouldn't I have my own?

"Of course, for formal use and entertaining the coupe or that delightfully intimate four-passenger Victoria might be more practical, but our seven-passenger sedan—it's a "400" too—takes care of our social needs and evening parties most admirably."

Notable features of the 1930 Nash "400" include: *Cable-actuated 4-wheel brakes, automatic chassis lubrication, built-in automatic radiator shutters, hydraulic shock absorbers, steel spring covers with sealed-in lifetime lubrication—and in the Twin-Ignition "8" Duplate non-shatterable plate glass throughout.*

(DEALER'S NAME)

1930 NASH "400"

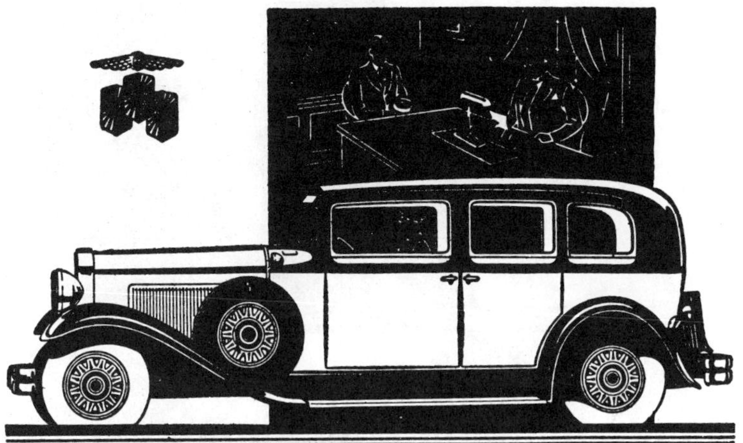

THE BANKER SPEAKS!

"WE bankers divide people into two classes—those who meet their obligations completely and those who don't.

"I have always found that my Nash car will do everything the engineers claim for it. That is why I drive a Nash '400.'

"It gives me all the prestige my position demands, and it returns the utmost for the money invested.

"It's comfortable, and it's smart, and I find it more economical than any other car in the same price class. Two extra miles per gallon doesn't seem like a great saving, but compounded for a year, it makes a substantial dividend. Long training has taught me to spend money carefully and *only* when it promises satisfactory returns.

"I am more than satisfied with my Nash investment."

Notable Twin-Ignition Eight features include: *New Straight-Eight, Twin-Ignition, Valve-in-head engine—9-bearing crankshaft—centralized chassis lubrication—Built-in automatic radiator shutters—hydraulic shock absorbers—Duplate non-shatterable plate glass throughout—steel spring covers with sealed-in lifetime lubrication*

(DEALER'S NAME)

1930 NASH "400"

THE ARTIST SPEAKS!

"LIKE all artists, I love beauty wherever I find it. Graceful contours and harmonious colors make a deep appeal to me. That is one reason why I was drawn to the new Nash '400' the moment I saw it.

"Every detail from the narrow rim radiator to rear bumper suggests the inspired effort of true artists who have sought and found a distinctive design which is both simple and dignified.

"Since I have owned a Nash, I have learned that there is more than surface beauty in this car. The rhythm of twin-ignition performance, the ease of steering, and the luxurious body comfort are in themselves a constant source of delight."

Notable Twin-Ignition Eight features include: ***Famous Twin-Ignition engine with 16 spark plugs—centralized chassis lubrication—built-in automatic radiator shutters—hydraulic shock absorbers—Duplate non-shatterable plate glass throughout—steel spring covers—etc.***

(DEALER'S NAME)

1930 NASH "400"

AN ENGINEER SPEAKS!

"I DROVE one of the first cars Nash ever built. That was thirteen years ago. It was a good car then . . . I have learned a lot about motor cars in thirteen years, and I am driving a 1930 Nash '400' now.

"Good engineering, after all, is simply that knowledge which enables men to select the best materials and combine them with the best processes to do a given task.

"I have made a careful study of each new Nash feature as it was introduced. I have gone over every inch of the new straight-eight chassis from the twin-ignition, valve-in-head engine to the hydraulic shock absorbers and centralized lubricating system. I have been especially impressed with the easy steering mechanism and with the positive action of the four-wheel brakes. Each improvement seems a definite step towards mechanical perfection.

"I know that Nash never adds a new feature 'just to be different'. A proven engineering principle always lies back of it.

"Personally, I don't believe there is a better designed car on the market today."

Notable Twin-Ignition Eight features include: *New Straight Eight, Twin-Ignition, Valve-in-head engine—9-bearing crankshaft—centralized chassis lubrication—built-in automatic radiator shutters—hydraulic shock absorbers—Duplate non-shatterable plate glass throughout—etc.*

(DEALER'S NAME)

1930 NASH "400"

THE SPORTSMAN SPEAKS!

"WHEN I drive, I want action. In my new Nash '400' Twin-Ignition Eight, I get it.!

"Not being an engineer I can't explain all the reasons for twin-ignition superiority, but I feel it every time I touch the throttle. This car's performance satisfies me at every speed.

"What I want in a motor car is a responsive engine, ample power, easy steering, road balance, and above all, endurance—ability to stand hard usage—and that's what I get in my Nash, with surprisingly little expense.

"Of course, I admire the slim grace of the Nash body lines, too. No man today forgets that a handsome car is a social asset."

Notable Twin-Ignition Eight features include: *New Straight Eight, Twin-Ignition, Valve-in-head engine—9-bearing crankshaft—centralized chassis lubrication—built-in automatic radiator shutters—hydraulic shock absorbers—Duplate non-shatterable plate glass throughout—etc.*

(DEALER'S NAME)

1930 NASH "400"

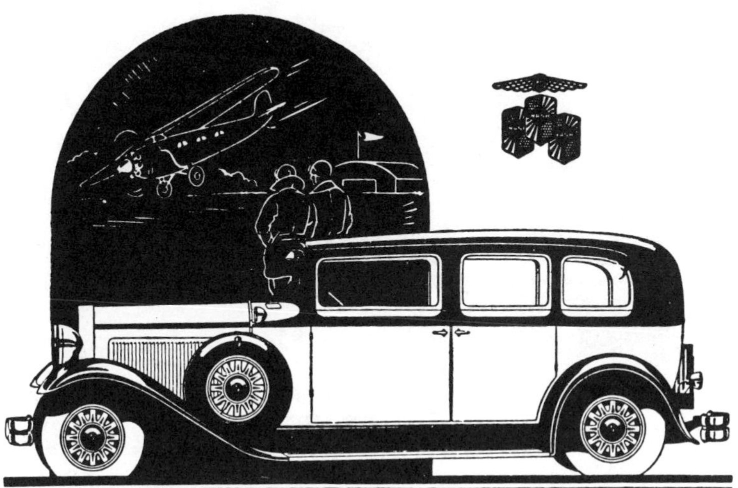

AN AVIATOR SPEAKS!

"AN aviator has to know engines intimately—his life often depends upon their performance.

"It was an excellent idea to apply the Twin-Ignition principle to pleasure cars. It means an added superiority of performance that can not be too highly praised.

"Of course, we are used to twin ignition in air engines, but the first time I drove that easy steering, beautifully balanced Nash '400,' I must confess that it seemed even smoother than my airplane.

"Performance is the first thing a flyer wants in a plane or a car, but pleasing lines and colors mean something too.

"Personally, I don't believe there is a better looking car on the market than the new Nash '400' for 1930."

Notable features of the 1930 Nash "400" include: *Cable-actuated 4-wheel brakes, automatic chassis lubrication, built-in automatic radiator shutters, hydraulic shock absorbers, world's easiest steering—steel spring covers with sealed-in lifetime lubrication*—and in the Twin Ignition "8" *Duplate non-shatterable plate glass throughout.*

(DEALER'S NAME)

1930 NASH "400"

THE DOCTOR SPEAKS!

"TWO o'clock in the morning is no time for delays. When I step on the starter the engine must respond... instantly!

"I drive a NASH '400' because I am a doctor... not a mechanic. My job is to attend human ills... I can't be bothered with engine trouble.

"The Nash Twin-Ignition principle first attracted me. It is an idea that would appeal to the precision instinct of any scientific mind. Two spark plugs naturally work better than one... like two hands, two eyes, two ears.

"That's the reason for my supreme confidence in the NASH '400.' Almost every night I have an emergency call ... and my Nash has never failed me.

"I trust this motor car as I do my professional implements."

Notable Twin-Ignition Eight features include: *New Straight Eight, Twin-Ignition, Valve-in-head engine—9-bearing crankshaft—Centralized chassis lubrication—Built-in automatic radiator shutters—hydraulic shock absorbers—Duplate non-shatterable plate glass throughout—etc.*

(DEALER'S NAME)

1930 NASH "400"

APPENDIX XII

"A Taste that Pleased the World"

Obtaining world-wide acceptance for a food product is no easy matter. Many manufacturers have failed. Practically all have gone through years of "red letter" experimentation. Success, when it came, was bought at a very high price.

Food advertising abroad has always been considered a difficult problem. Acceptance of food depends, to a great extent, upon appetite. In America we like and eat great quantities of ice-cream. Millions who live abroad wouldn't think of touching this favored confection of ours. Appetities, as a rule, vary with the latitudes. National tastes are as different as topographies.

Because there is a real magnitude to the task of marketing a food product abroad, it may be interesting to follow the procedure of one of America's most successful food product exporters—the Kellogg Company of Battle Creek, Michigan. No other example could be more typical. Certainly, few products have been started on their way with greater difficulties to overcome.

Kellogg products are ready-to-eat cereals. What European or Asiatic ever heard of a ready-to-eat cereal for breakfast? To try forcing this uniquely American food upon the foreigner seemed extremely foolhardy, and certainly would have been but for the fact that a careful study of the project was made and plans were complete years in advance before a single line of advertising was released.

The Kellogg Company began its careful program of foreign advertising eight years ago. When the Kellogg campaign began, ready-to-eat cereal was unknown to the Briton. Last year it took hundreds of thousands of packages to satisfy his appetite. In France, South America, and Central America the established custom of coffee and rolls for breakfast is rapidly giving way to corn flakes and other Kellogg cereals. Furthermore these cereals are now eaten abroad for luncheon, dinner, supper, as well as breakfast.

Today Kellogg advertising appears in the magazines and newspapers of twenty-seven different foreign countries. The best hotels and restaurants in all these countries stock the products. "Kellogg" is a name known around the world. Today's advertising activity—although not without its problems—is comparatively easy. People are much the same regardless of where they live. All of us feel that anything which has universal acceptance must be good. Kellogg's has it. Present advertising continually reiterates that point—"12,000,000 users daily."

But eight years ago the situation was entirely different. The easy selling-points that now continually react to Kellogg's advantage had to be worked for and planned with infinite pains.

Cautiously, Kellogg's was placed on the market. Sales were carefully checked. Reactions of various countries were tabulated. If the products were favorably received, what was the reason? A review showed that everybody liked the taste. That was something no one could forecast, something no one expected, for taste has never been a thing upon which the world was supposed to agree. Yet figures proved the point indisputably, and because of painstaking care and research Kellogg had an advertising point of unusual excellence. That combination of salt, sugar, and malt employed as flavoring pleased the palate of Briton and Mexican, Australian and Japanese. It was a universal point of agreement.

The next step was to coordinate that happy attribute of "a taste that pleased the world" with another outstanding feature, one that formed the keynote of domestic sales—the fact that Kellogg products are extremely healthful. The greatest thing in the world is health, and so health was advertised to the world. Such were the steps that led up to the forming of the Kellogg foreign advertising policy as it is today. The backbone of every campaign is health and taste. These are two things in which the universe is interested. Kellogg advertising never strays from these fundamentals and, consequently, every piece of copy is of equal interest to the residents of Tokio and London, Bombay and Paris.

The 1930 series of Kellogg export advertisements clearly indicate the influence of a definite plan and purpose. Each piece of copy and every layout hews to the line. These advertisements also show that work being done in the foreign field compares most favorably, from every standpoint, with that which is prepared for domestic readers.

The illustrations are simple, yet all the more striking because of it. Most noteworthy is the fact that they indicate a knowledge, on the part of the artist, of export requirements. Where figures are used, no national characteristics of dress or mannerisms are allowed to creep in and spoil the localized atmosphere which is of such great aid to the pulling power of any advertisement. Figures seem purposely drawn in the simplest possible fashion.

If a woman appears as a part of an illustration, she looks like a señorita when the text is in Spanish, yet might just as readily be a belle from Brisbane when the advertisement appears in English with an Australian imprint. This is a real achievement, especially evident to those who are close to export advertising and remember some of the incongruities that constantly cropped up during the good old days when ignorance was bliss.

The method of handling the Kellogg export advertising is equally efficient and "foreign-minded." The advertisements are made up in a number of standard sizes so that the needs of magazines and newspapers abroad may be complied with no matter what the requirements may be.

The Surprise that Sharpens Appetites

You don't need to see Rice Krispies in order to recognize them. So crisp and crunchy is this new cereal made by Kellogg that you can actually hear it snap . . . crackle . . . pop when you pour on cold milk or cream. A fine sound for sharpening appetites!

Kellogg's Rice Krispies are choice grains of rice—toasted into brown bubbles; they taste delicious, indescribably so! Good for everybody and simple to serve, no cooking required. Use them in soups, for macaroons—in a dozen ways! Order a red-and-green packet from the grocer and see how the whole family devour them!

RICE KRISPIES

Kellogg Company of Great Britain, Ltd.
329 High Holborn, London, W. C. 1

Made in Canada, 8½d a packet.

601

Tempts the taste of growing children

MILLIONS of mothers have found a friend in Kellogg's Corn Flakes—they have a flavour children can't resist. And so nourishing, too! Wholesome... crisp ...easy to digest. Serve with cold milk or cream. No cooking necessary. Fruits or honey may be added for variety.

An excellent breakfast cereal, of course... and an ideal dish for in-between meals or dessert. Enjoyed by young and old alike.

Insist on Kellogg's—the original corn flakes—with the flavour that cannot be copied. Always oven-fresh. Sold by all grocers in the red-and-green packet.

DEALER'S NAME

Also makers of Kellogg's ALL-BRAN – a laxative food

Index

Titles in This Series

1.
Henry Foster Adams. Advertising and Its Mental Laws. 1916

2.
Advertising Research Foundation. Copy Testing. 1939

3.
Hugh E. Agnew. Outdoor Advertising. 1938

4.
Earnest Elmo Calkins. And Hearing Not: Annals of an Ad Man. 1946

5.
Earnest Elmo Calkins and Ralph Holden. Modern Advertising. 1905

6.
John Caples. Advertising Ideas: A Practical Guide to Methods That Make Advertisements Work. 1938

7.
Jean-Louis Chandon. A Comparative Study of Media Exposure Models. 1985

8.
Paul Terry Cherington. The Consumer Looks at Advertising. 1928

9.
C. Samuel Craig and Avijit Ghosh, editors. The Development of Media Models in Advertising: An Anthology of Classic Articles. 1985

10.
C. Samuel Craig and Brian Sternthal, editors. Repetition Effects Over the Years: An Anthology of Classic Articles. 1985

11.
John K. Crippen. Successful Direct-Mail Methods. 1936

12.
Ernest Dichter. The Strategy of Desire. 1960

13.
Ben Duffy. Advertising Media and Markets. 1939

14.
Warren Benson Dygert. Radio as an Advertising Medium. 1939

15.
Francis Reed Eldridge. Advertising and Selling Abroad. 1930

16.
J. George Frederick, editor. Masters of Advertising Copy: Principles and Practice of Copy Writing According to its Leading Practitioners. 1925

17.
George French. Advertising: The Social and Economic Problem. 1915

18.
Max A. Geller. Advertising at the Crossroads: Federal Regulation vs. Voluntary Controls. 1952

19.
Avijit Ghosh and C. Samuel Craig. The Relationship of Advertising Expenditures to Sales: An Anthology of Classic Articles. 1985

20.
Albert E. Haase. The Advertising Appropriation, How to Determine It and How to Administer It. 1931

21.
S. Roland Hall. The Advertising Handbook, 1921

22.
S. Roland Hall. Retail Advertising and Selling. 1924

23.
Harry Levi Hollingworth. Advertising and Selling: Principles of Appeal and Response. 1913

24.
Floyd Y. Keeler and Albert E. Haase. The Advertising Agency, Procedure and Practice. 1927

25.
H. J. Kenner. The Fight for Truth in Advertising. 1936

26.
Otto Kleppner. Advertising Procedure. 1925

27.
Harden Bryant Leachman. The Early Advertising Scene. 1949

28.
E. St. Elmo Lewis. Financial Advertising, for Commercial and Savings Banks, Trust, Title Insurance, and Safe Deposit Companies, Investment Houses. 1908

29.
R. Bigelow Lockwood. Industrial Advertising Copy. 1929

30.
D. B. Lucas and C. E. Benson. Psychology for Advertisers. 1930

31.
Darrell B. Lucas and Steuart H. Britt. Measuring Advertising Effectiveness. 1963

32.
Papers of the American Association of Advertising Agencies. 1927

33.
Printer's Ink. Fifty Years 1888–1938. 1938

34.
Jason Rogers. Building Newspaper Advertising. 1919

35.
George Presbury Rowell. Forty Years an Advertising Agent, 1865–1905. 1906

36.
Walter Dill Scott. The Theory of Advertising: A Simple Exposition of the Principles of Psychology in Their Relation to Successful Advertising. 1903

37.
Daniel Starch. Principles of Advertising. 1923

38.
Harry Tipper, George Burton Hotchkiss, Harry L. Hollingworth, and Frank Alvah Parsons. Advertising, Its Principles and Practices. 1915

39.
Roland S. Vaile. Economics of Advertising. 1927

40.
Helen Woodward. Through Many Windows. 1926